D0441433

WOODROW WILSON

Revolution, War, and Peace

Arthur S. Link

*George Henry Davis '86 Professor of
American History, and Director and Editor of
The Papers of Woodrow Wilson,
Princeton University*

AHM Publishing Corporation

Arlington Heights, Illinois 60004

ISBN 0-88295-799-6, cloth
ISBN 0-88295-798-8, paper

Library of Congress Catalog Number: 79-50909

PRINTED IN THE UNITED STATES OF AMERICA
7129
Second Printing

For Margaret Douglas Link

Collaborator for thirty-four years

Contents

Preface

This book, originally written as the Albert Shaw Lectures on Diplomatic History at The Johns Hopkins University, was first published by the Johns Hopkins University Press in 1957 under the title, *Wilson the Diplomatist: A Look at His Major Foreign Policies.* It was reprinted in 1963 with a "Preface to the Second Edition," which corrected certain errors in the first printing.

When the opportunity arose to publish a new edition of the book, I originally planned to make only minor changes in the text. However, when I read the book in its entirety for the first time since 1962, I discovered that I, and numerous scholars working in the period, had learned many new things and had had many new insights about Wilson and his diplomatic policies since *Wilson the Diplomatist* was first published. Thus I rewrote the book. I was able to use small portions of the old book, particularly the account of Wilson's western tour in 1919. However, this is substantially a new book with new themes. They are embodied in the new title, for Wilson was the first President of the modern era to confront all the difficult problems of revolution, war, and peace.

Whether *Woodrow Wilson: Revolution, War, and Peace* represents a more mature understanding of Wilson the diplomatist and the legacy that he left us than was displayed in the original book, only my readers will be able to determine.

I am grateful to John Milton Cooper, Jr., William H. Harbaugh, David W. Hirst, and Richard W. Leopold for reading my manuscript with understanding and care, and for their helpful suggestions and criticisms. My wife, Margaret Douglas Link, was, as always, my best editor. Professor Harbaugh also made many suggestions for stylistic improvements. I alone am responsible for the final content and opinions expressed in this book. I thank Harlan Davidson, president of the AHM Publishing Corporation, for his constant encouragement and support.

ARTHUR S. LINK

Princeton University
December 5, 1978

I

Wilson the Diplomatist

A man of serious mien walked to the stands outside the east front of the Capitol on March 4, 1913, to take the oath as twenty-eighth President of the United States. He was Woodrow Wilson, born in Staunton, Virginia, on December 29, 1856, educated at Davidson College and Princeton University, trained in law at the University of Virginia, and prepared for teaching and scholarship in political science and history at The Johns Hopkins University. From 1885 to 1902 he taught successively at Bryn Mawr College, Wesleyan University, The Johns Hopkins University, and Princeton University. After his election to the presidency of the latter institution in 1902, he transformed a venerable if run-down college into a modern university. Meanwhile, he became embroiled in a personal controversy with the Dean of the Graduate School over control of that school and the location of a residential graduate college and escaped the troubled Princeton scene by accepting nomination for the governorship of New Jersey in 1910. He was elected, and, with irresistible power, captured the Democratic presidential nomination and the presidency of the United States itself in 1912.

Wilson guided the destinies of his country through eight of the most critical years of the modern epoch. The period of his presidency, 1913 to 1921, was a time at home of far-reaching attempts to resolve the problems created by the existence of large uncontrolled private economic interests in a political and social democracy. For the world at large, it was a time of revolutionary upheaval, cataclysmic world war, and shifts in the balance of power that threatened the very foundations of the international order.

As a domestic leader, who articulated American democratic traditions and used the resources of party and presidential leadership to devise and achieve solutions for the problems raised by twentieth-century economic and social developments, Wilson succeeded so well that he earned an undisputed place among the first rank of Presidents. As a leader in foreign affairs, who guided the American people from provincialism toward world leadership and responsibilities, Wilson's accomplishments were even more significant for the long future than his achievements in domestic affairs.

Wilson came to the presidency with better training for the conduct of foreign affairs than any Chief Executive since John Quincy Adams. He had thorough grounding in international law, modern history, and comparative systems of government; and he taught all these subjects with increasing effectiveness and some distinction after 1885. His knowledge of these fields, and particularly his disciplined habit of looking at events with a self-conscious effort to take a detached, long view of them and put them in historical perspective, would stand him in good stead when, as President, he had to confront momentous questions of policy. Over and over—during crises with Mexico and Germany before 1917 and during the period of American belligerency and the Paris Peace Conference—Wilson tried to take the long historical view and to persuade others to follow his example. On numerous occasions he said that he was playing for the verdict of history. As he put it in a conversation with Ida Tarbell in 1916:

> In handling national affairs feeling must never take precedence of judgment. I used to tell my students long before I had an idea of going into politics that no case could ever be made up at the time it was developing. The final judgment on everything that happens in the world will be made up long years after the happening—that is, the student always has the last say. He interprets the letters, the documents. I have tried to look at this war ten years ahead, to be a historian at the same time I was an actor. A hundred years from now it will not be the bloody details that the world will think of in this war: it will be the causes behind it, the readjustments which it will force.

Before his entry into public life, Wilson, as scholar and analyst, had concentrated on domestic politics in the Anglo-American tradition. In his first and best-known book, *Congressional Government* (1885), Wilson made only a passing reference to foreign affairs. In *The State* (1889), an excellent pioneer textbook in comparative government, he gave only a page and a half to international law in a total of more than one hundred pages devoted to the development of law and legal institutions. Moreover, in his summary chapters on the functions and objects of government, he placed foreign relations at the bottom of his list of the "constituent functions." He then elaborated the functions and objects of government and did not even mention the conduct of external affairs!

Wilson began to evidence keen interest in foreign affairs for the first time in the late 1890s and early 1900s. He was reacting in part to new shifts in international power then in process. He was also reacting to changes in American thinking about the future role of the United States in world affairs as a consequence of the Venezuelan controversy with Great Britain, the war with Spain, the extension of American interests to the Far East, and the acquisition of an overseas empire. The war with Spain, he wrote in his *History of the American People* (1902), had been only one sign of a more important underlying development—the end of American isolation and the inevitable beginning of a new era in which the United States would have to play a widening role in world politics. It followed inexorably, Wilson added in an essay "Democracy and Efficiency," that Americans were living in a new and more perilous time in which changed circumstances had rendered meaningless and dangerous their time-encrusted traditions of self-sufficiency and security through isolation. The American people, he concluded, were now neighbors to the world, whether they liked it or not, and could not escape the coming challenges by ignoring them.

Wilson also saw clearly that the sudden emergence of the United States to world power would have a profound and enduring impact upon the balance of authority and leadership in the federal government. "Much the most important change to be noticed," he wrote in the preface to the fifteenth printing of *Congressional Government* in 1900, "is the result of the war with Spain upon the lodgment and exercise of power within our federal system: the greatly increased power and opportunity for constructive statesmanship given the President, by the plunge into international politics and into the administration of distant dependencies, which has been that war's most striking and momentous consequence."

Wilson's last book, *Constitutional Government in the United States* (1908), reiterated these themes:

> The war with Spain again changed the balance of parts. Foreign questions became leading questions again, as they had been in the first days of the government, and in them the President was of necessity leader. Our new place in the affairs of the world has since that year of transformation kept him at the front of our government, where our own thoughts and the attention of men everywhere is centred upon him. . . . Our President can never again be the mere domestic figure he has been throughout so large a part of our history. The nation has risen to the first rank in power and resources. . . . Our President must always, henceforth, be one of the great powers of the world, whether he act greatly and wisely or not. . . . We have but begun to see the presidential office in this light; but it is the light which will more and more beat upon it, and more and more determine its character and its effect upon the politics of the nation.

Wilson faced foreign problems of greater magnitude during his tenure in the White House than any President since the early years of the nineteenth century. He carried out policies, whether wisely or unwisely, that were firmly grounded upon a consistent body of principles and assumptions that supplied motive power and shaped policy in the fields of action in diplomacy as well as domestic policy. These principles and assumptions were deeply rooted in Wilson's general thinking about God, ethics, the nature and ends of government, and the role of the United States in advancing democracy and the cause of human rights throughout the world. These principles and assumptions were in turn enlarged and refined as Wilson sought to apply them in particular situations.

The foundations of Wilson's political thinking were the beliefs and ethical values that he inherited from the Christian tradition in general and from Presbyterianism in particular. Indeed, it is not too much to say that his Christian faith informed and influenced his every action and policy. Wilson was almost like a child in his faith: He never doubted, always believed, and sought guidance and strength for daily life from reading the Bible, church attendance, and prayer. He derived his faith from his father, the Rev. Dr. Joseph Ruggles Wilson, a Presbyterian minister, and from the Westminster Confession and the Shorter Catechism. Hence Wilson was, inevitably, a Calvinist. He believed in a sovereign God, just but also loving; in a moral universe, the laws of which ruled nations as well as men; in the supreme revelation of Jesus Christ; and in the Bible as the incomparable word of God and the rule of life. He further believed that God controls history and uses men and nations to achieve His preordained purposes.

A second main theme in Wilson's political thinking with large implications for his foreign policy was his belief in democracy as the most advanced, humane, and, in the long run, most effective form of government. From the beginning to the end of his adult career, he studied, wrote about, and put into practice the essential aspects of democratic government. This is not the place to review his splendid synthesis of Anglo-American democratic theories and traditions. However, it is important to understand how these determinative political beliefs helped to form his objectives and to shape his policies in foreign affairs.

Everything depended upon Wilson's view of the nature and capacities of humankind. He believed that all peoples were capable of self-government because all were endowed with inherent character and capacity for growth. He was too good a student of history to be visionary in these beliefs. He repudiated and condemned utopianism and taught that people learn democracy only by long years of disciplined experience. As early as 1885, we hear him saying:

> Democracy is, of course, wrongly conceived when treated as merely a body of doctrine. It is a stage of development. It is not created by aspirations or by new faith; it is built up by slow habit. Its process is experience, its basis old wont, its meaning national organic oneness and effectual life. It comes, like manhood, as the fruit of youth: immature peoples cannot have it, and the maturity to which it is vouchsafed is the maturity of freedom and self-control, and no other.

Even so, Wilson deeply believed that all peoples, whether Mexican peons or Russian peasants, whites, blacks, or Orientals, were capable in the long run of being trained or self-trained in the disciplines of democracy and of learning to govern themselves. "When properly directed," he said in 1914, "there is no people not fitted for self-government."

Inevitably, these assumptions had profound implications for Wilson's thought about the development and relationships of nations. His belief in the capacity of man, in progress as the organic law of life and the working out of the divine plan in history, and in democracy as the highest form of government fired in him the hope that democracy would some day be the universal rule of political life.

The final main assumptions of Wilson's thoughts about international relations grew out of his attempt to define the role of the United States in world affairs within the context of American democratic traditions and his own political and religious faith. He believed that the American people had a peculiar role to play in history, precisely because they were in many ways unique among the peoples of the world. They were unique *politically,* he believed, not because they alone possessed democratic institutions, but because they had succeeded in organizing diverse sections and a hundred million people into a federal system such as one day (he at last conceived) might provide a model for a world organization. The American people were unique *socially,* first, because of their radical affirmation of equality and their emphatic repudiation of everything for which the caste- and class-ridden societies of Europe and Asia stood. Americans were unique socially, in the second place, because they were a new people, the product of the mixing of all races of the world. Finally, they were unique *morally.* The United States, Wilson believed, had been born that men might be free. Americans had done more than any other people to advance human welfare. Americans, above all other peoples, were, as he put it, "custodians of the spirit of righteousness, of the spirit of equal-handed justice, of the spirit of hope which believes in the perfectibility of the law with the perfectibility of human life itself."

Thus America's mission in the world was not to attain wealth and power, but to serve mankind through leadership in moral purposes and in advancing peace and world unity. As he himself put it in a poetic outburst during the preconvention campaign of 1912:

> There is a spirit that rules us. If I did not believe in Providence I would feel like a man going blindfolded through a haphazard world. I do believe in Providence. I believe that God presided over the inception of this nation; I believe that God planted in us the vision of liberty; I believe that men are emancipated in proportion as they lift themselves to the conception of Providence and of divine destiny, and, therefore, I cannot be deprived of the hope that is in me—in the hope not only that concerns myself, but the confident hope that concerns the nation—that we are chosen, and prominently chosen, to show the way to the nations of the world how they shall walk in the paths of liberty.

This is not to suggest that Wilson was oblivious to the economic realities behind foreign policy, or that he did not think about the necessity of a nation having well-defined international economic policies and goals. As N. Gordon Levin, Jr., has pointed out in his *Woodrow Wilson and World Politics* (1968), Wilson believed, as did most of his thoughtful contemporaries, that, on account of the ending of the frontier, American prosperity in the twentieth century would in large measure depend upon the expansion of American overseas exports and investments. Moreover, as Carl P. Parrini has said in his *Heir to Empire: United States Economic Diplomacy, 1916–1923* (1969), the foundations of modern American international economic policy were solidly laid by the Wilson administration.

In devising international economic policy, however, Wilson and his advisers operated well within the boundaries that were firmly set by their conception of the historic mission of the United States. This Wilsonian international economic policy, if such it may be called, included the promotion of international trade through a general lowering of tariff walls, a destruction of all systems of monopoly and special privileges, and, above all, a fair field with *no* favors, as much for Americans as for Japanese, Englishmen, or Frenchmen. This was of course the historic conception of the Open Door, but it was an Open Door that was to be employed, not for the oppressive exploitation of underdeveloped areas, but for the slow and steady improvement of mankind through the spread of a reformed and socially responsible democratic capitalism. There is not a single instance on record when Wilson ever sought to obtain for any American citizen monopolistic concessions or preferential treatment in investment and trade.

Christian humanism and a deep personal commitment to human rights, liberty, and the right of peoples to govern themselves all combined to produce other fundamental beliefs that profoundly affected Wilson's foreign policies and his conduct of foreign relations.

First, he utterly detested the exploitative imperialist system that had reached its zenith by 1913. The fact that financiers and investors, with the backing of their governments, worked through puppet or cooperative governments to exploit the peoples of underdeveloped countries was anathema to him. He stated his feeling clearly in a speech in 1914:

> The Department of State at Washington is constantly called upon to back up the commercial enterprises and the industrial enterprises of the United States in foreign countries, and it at one time went so far in that direction that all its diplomacy came to be designated as "dollar diplomacy." It was called upon to support every man who wanted to earn anything, anywhere, if he was an American. But there ought to be a limit to that. There is no man who is more interested than I am in carrying the enterprise of American businessmen to every quarter of the globe. I was interested in it long before I was suspected of being a politician. I have been preaching it year after year as the great thing that lay in the future for the United States—to show her wit and skill and enterprise and influence in every country in the world. But observe the limit to all that which is laid upon us, perhaps more than upon any other nation in the world. We set this nation up, at any rate we professed to set it up, to vindicate the rights of men. We did not name any differences between one race and another. We did not set up any barriers against any particular people. We opened our gates to all the world and said: "Let all men who wish to be free come to us and they will be welcome." We said, "This independence of ours is not a selfish

thing for our own exclusive private use. It is for everybody to whom we can find the means of extending it." We cannot, with that oath taken in our youth, we cannot with that great ideal set before us when we were a young people and numbered only a scant three millions, take upon ourselves, now that we are a hundred million strong, any other conception of duty than we then entertained. If American enterprise in foreign countries, particularly in those foreign countries which are not strong enough to resist us, takes the shape of imposing upon and exploiting the mass of the people of that country, it ought to be checked and not encouraged. I am willing to get anything for an American that money and enterprise can obtain except the suppression of the rights of other men. I will not help any man buy a power which he ought not to exercise over fellow beings.

Wilson did not limit his action to speech making. He was the first effective antiimperialist statesman of the twentieth century. He broke up a six-power consortium of bankers which had obtained concessions that threatened the political independence of China. He singlehandedly turned back Japanese aggression against China's independence in 1915. At the Paris Peace Conference, he forced the Japanese to promise to surrender to China administrative and political control of Shantung Province, which Japan had seized from Germany—a promise which the Japanese government honored in 1922. Again, almost singlehandedly, Wilson directly attacked and destroyed the imperialistic system in Mexico, where it had reached its apex. He then defended the Mexican Revolution against European intervention, foiled the efforts of American investors to support counterrevolutionary movements, insisted upon the right of the Mexican people to control their land and mineral and oil resources, and enabled the Mexicans to move forward in their own way toward self-government and freedom from outside control. As he explained to his Secretary of War, who in 1914 was insisting upon military intervention:

I have your letter of this morning and understand perfectly the motives and the sense of duty which led you to write it.

But my judgment remains unaltered and I want you to know why.

9

We shall have no right at any time to intervene in Mexico to determine the way in which the Mexicans are to settle their own affairs. I feel sufficiently assured that the property and lives of foreigners will not suffer in the process of the settlement. The rest is political and Mexican. Many things may happen of which we do not approve and which could not happen in the United States, but I say very solemnly that that is no affair of ours. Our responsibility will come after the settlement and in the determination of the question whether the new government is to receive the recognition of the Government of the United States or not. There are in my judgment no conceivable circumstances which would make it right for us to direct by force or by threat of force the internal processes of what is a profound revolution, a revolution as profound as that which occurred in France. All the world has been shocked ever since the time of the revolution in France that Europe should have undertaken to nullify what was done there, no matter what the excesses then committed.

I speak very solemnly but with clear judgment in the matter, which I hope God will give me strength to act upon.

Second, Wilson's strong belief in self-determination and his detestation of what Gordon Levin has called atavistic (predatory) imperialism combined to produce the first effective decolonizer among the statesmen of the twentieth century. Between 1913 and 1916, he did everything within his legal authority to increase the participation of the Filipino people in their own government. Meanwhile, he kept steady pressure on Congress to enact a new organic act for the Philippine Islands. It came in the form of the Jones Act of 1916, which granted almost complete autonomy to the Philippines. He also supported the Clarke Amendment to that act, which promised early independence. It passed the Senate but was defeated in the House by northeastern Democrats who joined the measure's Republican opponents under pressure of the Roman Catholic hierarchy. Wilson continued to push and won passage of the Jones Act of 1917, which granted territorial status to Puerto Rico and American citizenship to the inhabitants of that island. Wilson put heavy pressure on British leaders at the Paris Peace Conference to grant self-government to Ireland. The mandate system, embodied in the Covenant of the

League of Nations for the governance of former German colonies and Ottoman provinces, was largely Wilson's idea and handiwork. By establishing the principle that these territories were to be governed exclusively in the interests of their own inhabitants, Wilson eventually spelled the doom of territorial imperialism, long though that result was in coming.

Wilson as a decolonizer and advocate of the right of self-determination was no visionary idealist. For example, he believed that the Austro-Hungarian Empire served a vital purpose in maintaining the economic and political unity of Central Europe. Hence he tried hard to maintain that empire on a basis of autonomy for its subject peoples. He was the last major Allied leader to recognize the Czech National Council; there was nothing that he could have done to prevent the Hapsburg realm from coming apart at the seams. However, at Paris, he won treaties and agreements for the internationalization of the Danube River, the protection of the rights of minorities in the successor states, and so on.

Third, Christian ethics and generous compassion fostered in Wilson an abhorrence of violence, particularly of war, as a means of settling international disputes. Wilson had no killer instinct, in fact, he is not known ever to have committed a single act of personal violence in his life. He never hunted; his brother-in-law has said that he could not even cut off a chicken's head. Wilson said over and over that no war (except the Civil War, which preserved the Union) had ever resulted in any lasting good. Hence his consistent advocacy of treaties of conciliation and arbitration, and particularly of the provisions of the Convenant of the League of Nations aimed at preventing aggression short of war.

Yet, Wilson was in no sense an absolute pacifist. He believed that force had been and was a last legitimate resort against unendurable aggression, oppression, and tyranny. He once said that Americans in 1776 had struck a blow for the liberty of all mankind. He went to war with Germany in 1917 because he believed that he had no alternative, and also because he believed that American participation would hasten the end of the war. He also included a provision in the League of Nations Covenant for united military action against an aggressor once all other recourses had failed.

As he revealed in his letter to the Secretary of War in 1914, he believed that revolutions were justified when people had no other means of seeking redress against oppression. He rejoiced over the Russian Revolution of March 1917; then, following the triumph of the Bolsheviks, he insisted that the revolution was inevitable after centuries of czarist oppression.

As a corollary, he learned (the hard way in Mexico, after the occupation of Veracruz in April 1914) that it was (so he believed) futile, even foolish, to attempt to turn back the force of a profound social and economic revolution. After Veracruz, he insisted upon the right of Mexicans to settle their own affairs. Finally, in 1918 and 1919 he rebuffed the grandiose and fatuous plans of the British and French to defeat the Bolsheviks by wholesale military intervention.

Only a confirmed cynic will deny that a large measure of Wilson's strength as a diplomatist and much of his contributions to the field of international relations originated from his spiritual resources. There were even *practical* advantages in idealism. By rejecting selfish, narrow nationalism and materialism as bases for foreign policy, and by articulating the noblest traditions of western culture, Wilson could and did speak with universal authority. Ideals are a dynamic force in cultures that acknowledge their validity: Wilson was a more effective war leader, a more fearful antagonist of German military leaders on the ideological battlefield, and a more indomitable fighter for a just peace settlement precisely because he stood for what most men in the western world (including his enemies) were willing to acknowledge were their own highest ideals.

However, one cannot measure the significance of Wilson's idealism in practical terms alone. Societies degenerate into tyrannies of individuals, classes, or ideologies without ideals to recall past traditions and to provide guidance for the present and future. Wilson's greatest contributions were holding high humane traditions and the ideal of justice while hatreds and passions threatened to wreck Western civilization. By his rhetoric and moral power he not only rallied men of good will to the defense of these ideals; he also helped to save them for future generations.

Admittedly, Wilson's assumptions and principles to some degree impaired his leadership in the mundane affairs of state. His thinking, even more about foreign than about domestic matters, sometimes failed to take sufficient account of what specialists in international relations call "realities." The qualifying adjective *sufficient* is of vital significance. Wilson was never visionary, incapable of facing reality; on the contrary, he was keenly intelligent and often shrewd. He understood the beneficial effect of a balance of power among the great powers—to the point, in fact, that he wanted to preserve German power in Central Europe during and after the World War as a restraint on Russia and France. On the other hand, he had unbounded faith in the fundamental rationality and goodness of the common people—what he called "the organized opinion of mankind." As Arno Mayer has pointed out, it was the common people of western Europe who failed Wilson during the Paris Peace Conference.

Second, Wilson's uncommon concern about the fundamental principles of national and international life occasionally led him to oversimplify the complexities of international politics. He also had a tendency to invoke analogies between domestic and international politics without taking sufficient account of the enormous differences between the two. Thus he believed that the legal relations between nations should be the same as those subsisting between citizens of a single state. In other words, both sovereign nations and individuals should be subject to a common law. It was a noble ideal, just as noble as the medieval concept of the "Peace of God." However, it has been possible since Wilson's day to establish the rule of law only among nations that have similar political institutions and share common moral and political values.

We can gain much understanding of Wilson by looking at his techniques and methods as a diplomatist. They stemmed in part from his temperament. He was an intense activist who was never satisfied with "pale casts of thought." Driving force, relentless energy, and striving for definitive solutions characterized most of Wilson's efforts in the field of foreign affairs.

Mature conviction from scholarly study concerning the role that the President should play in the conduct of foreign relations also helped to determine Wilson's methods as a diplomatist. Even during the period when he emphasized congressional supremacy, Wilson recognized and pointed out the President's latitude in the conduct of affairs abroad. That recognition had grown into a sweeping affirmation of presidential sovereignty by the time that Wilson had matured in his thinking about the American constitutional system.

"One of the greatest of the President's powers," he said in *Constitutional Government in the United States,* "I have not yet spoken of at all: his control, which is very absolute, of the foreign relations of the nation. The initiative in foreign affairs, which the President possesses without any restriction whatever, is virtually the power to control them absolutely. The President cannot conclude a treaty with a foreign power without the consent of the Senate, but he may guide every step of diplomacy, and to guide diplomacy is to determine what treaties must be made, if the faith and prestige of the government are to be maintained. He need disclose no step of negotiation until it is complete, and when in any critical matter it is completed the government is virtually committed. Whatever its disinclination, the Senate may feel itself committed also."

These words offered a striking forecast of Wilson's own management of foreign affairs a few years later. In areas and about questions that he considered vitally important—the Far East, Mexico, relations with the European belligerents, wartime relations with the Allied powers, the problem of the Russian Revolution, and the writing of a peace settlement—Wilson exercised almost absolute personal control. To be sure, he listened to his advisers. His first Secretary of State, William Jennings Bryan, had great influence upon him, as did his second, Robert Lansing. Wilson also relied heavily on his most intimate informal adviser on foreign affairs, Colonel Edward M. House. Nevertheless, Wilson made all final decisions and personally conducted the diplomacy of the United States. He wrote most of the important diplomatic correspondence of the United States government on his own typewriter, sometimes bypassed the State Department by using his own private agents and advisers, and, occasionally, conducted important negotiations behind the backs of his secretaries of state. Moreover, in times of crisis he conducted diplomacy personally with the ambassadors and heads of missions in Washington. He also went in person as head of the American commission to the Paris Peace Conference.

Wilson took personal responsibility for the conduct of the important diplomacy of the United States, first, because he believed that it was wise, right, and necessary for him to do so. He believed that the people had temporarily vested their sovereignty in foreign affairs in him and that he could not delegate that solemn responsibility to any individual or department. His scholarly training and self-disciplined habits of work made him so much more efficient than his advisers that he concluded very early that the most economical way of doing important diplomatic business was to do it himself. Experience in dealing with subordinates who did not understand his purposes or tried to defeat them also led him to conclude that it was the safest method, for he deeply believed that he, and not his subordinates, bore the responsibility to the American people and to history for the consequences of his foreign policies.

Second, Wilson was President at a time when the structure of the executive branch was completely inadequate for its burdens. As President, Wilson had one assistant, Joseph Patrick Tumulty; a private stenographer, Charles Lee Swem; and a few typists in the Executive Office to acknowledge the routine mail that Wilson did not see. Wilson was equally shorthanded in the conduct of foreign relations. As compared to the Post Office, Treasury, and Interior departments, the State Department was one of the smaller departments of the federal government. It was comparable in size to the foreign offices of Latin American and small European states. Moreover, the State Department had no good system of intelligence. Yet by 1913 the United States was a great power and increasingly had to act like one. Lack of adequate personnel and his own temperament meant that much of the increasing burden of conducting foreign relations fell upon Wilson.

Third, Wilson often felt obliged to take personal control because many of his subordinates, from secretaries of state down to division chiefs in the Department of State and ambassadors and ministers, were poorly trained for their positions or incompetent. Bryan was appointed, not because he had any particular qualifications for the post, but because the administration had to have his support for its domestic program. In addition, it was difficult for Wilson to appoint experienced and able men as ambassadors and ministers because the Democratic party had been so long out of national power that it lacked a cadre of experienced personnel. For example, Wilson tried desperately to find what he called the best men for ambassadorships and to break the custom of using these offices as rewards for party service. Except in a few cases, the "best" men would not accept or could not afford to accept appointment, and Wilson had to yield to political pressures and name party hacks or wealthy men to important stations like Berlin, St. Petersburg, Rome, and Madrid.

Wilson was also encumbered with his quota of disloyal advisers and subordinates, and this was a fourth reason for his conviction that it was necessary for him to closely supervise all details of important foreign policy. This factor can be easily exaggerated. Bryan was the soul of loyalty and resigned when he could not follow his superior's policy with complete sincerity. Most other officers in the State Department and foreign service were faithful servants. Colonel House *usually* managed to suppress his overweening egotism and to represent Wilson loyally before 1919.

Wilson's greatest problem was Robert Lansing, Secretary of State from 1915 to 1920. Lansing, who looked every inch the statesman, was brilliant while executing routine business and often bungling while conducting important negotiations. A very bad blunder by Lansing in a controversy over armed ships in January 1916 first revealed the Secretary of State's ineptitude to Wilson and was one reason why Wilson increasingly refused to permit him to make any important decisions on his own. Worse still, the discussions over policy toward German submarine warfare in the spring of 1916 first made it apparent to Wilson that Lansing was trying to lead him into war. Lansing revealed this purpose even more clearly in the following autumn and winter. Since Wilson did not want to go to war, his distrust of Lansing naturally increased. Finally, Wilson lost all confidence in his Secretary of State when he tried to sabotage Wilson's efforts to end the war through mediation in December 1916 and January 1917. Unable to find a good replacement or to dismiss Lansing in the midst of various crises, Wilson thought that he had no recourse but to conduct all important negotiations himself. This isolation only increased Lansing's bitterness and tendency toward disloyalty, particularly during the peace conference and afterward. There is some evidence that Lansing contemplated a coup that would put him in the White House after Wilson's breakdown in October 1919. There is good evidence that Lansing tried to provoke a war with Mexico about the same time.

Wilson's critics have suggested a final reason for his techniques as a diplomatist—his personal egotism, jealousy of others, and inability ever to delegate authority. A search of the record does not yield much evidence to support these charges. A fairer conclusion would be that Wilson was generous in dealing with subordinates, welcomed and took advice, and often changed his mind. Indeed, Wilson's chief weakness as a diplomatist was his soft heart and unwillingness to dismiss incompetent and even disloyal subordinates. He could not do anything to embarrass or hurt another person. He finally dismissed Lansing in January 1920, but Lansing had done irreparable damage by then. Even though Wilson had good proof of House's disloyalty at Paris during the early stages of the peace negotiations, Wilson appointed the Colonel as his chief spokesman when he, Wilson, left the conference for a visit to the United States. House gave away most of Wilson's positions during the President's absence.

In the final reckoning, Wilson will be judged not so much by his thinking about foreign policy or his techniques as a diplomatist as by what he was able or unable to accomplish. No such pattern of almost unbroken success marked his record as a maker of foreign policy as it did of his record in domestic affairs. He failed to achieve many of the foreign policy objectives nearest to this heart. During the first two and a half years of the First World War he ardently desired to restore peace through his own mediation. He tried and failed. He sincerely hoped to keep his country from being sucked into the war's vortex. He tried and failed. He worked with incredible energy to construct a just and lasting peace settlement after the war. He did not succeed; at least he did not achieve all his objectives. Finally, he destroyed his health in an unsuccessful effort to persuade the Senate to consent to American membership in the League of Nations and to persuade the American people to take leadership in rebuilding the international community.

However, the world now honors Wilson most for his failures. It remembers the heroic and often lonely figure standing foursquare at Paris against forces of hatred, greed, and imperialism. It remembers the dauntless fighter stumping the country in an incredible and nearly fatal forensic effort. It remembers the man broken in health, but not in spirit, unyielding to what he thought was shameful compromise, confident that the sovereign Lord of history would turn all events into their appointed channels.

The passage of time—it is now more than half a century since Wilson left the White House—enables us to see Wilson and his contributions in the field of international relations with greater perspective than we once possessed. We have all lost our innocence about foreign affairs; we no longer expect either miracles or the millennium. What once seemed like Wilson's failures do not look altogether like failures now. Moreover, after the presidential disasters in foreign policy from Kennedy through Nixon, Wilson's decency and integrity—what might be summed up in the old-fashioned word "character"—make him look better and better. We are beginning to see that Wilson's achievements in the realm of foreign affairs were larger than we once thought and that he accomplished much even in momentary failure. Indeed, we are able to see that the passage of time has crystallized these achievements into legacies for our own time.

One of these achievements was Wilson's strong reaffirmation of the old American tradition of disinterested helpfulness to nations struggling toward self-government and a more abundant life. Cynics will smile and say that no great power can ever be altruistic in dealing with other nations, particularly small and helpless nations. They are of course right to some degree. If it is difficult for an individual to act in love and disinterestedness toward others, how much more difficult it is for nations to do so. However, it was Wilson's accomplishment that he proved it possible for great nations to assist small ones with some degree of altruism and success.

A second achievement was Wilson's vindication of the tradition that all peoples have the right, qualified only by their capacity to exercise it responsibly and without doing injury to others, to self-determination and self-government. Wilson achieved notable immediate and long-term successes in fighting for this tradition. His utterances during the war and afterward helped to destroy ancient empires based upon the subjugation of minority peoples. His success in establishing the mandate system helped to spell an end to old-fashioned imperialism and colonialism. His defense of the Mexican Revolution against European and American enemies made it possible for the Mexican people to hew out their own destiny. He stood off massive Allied intervention in the Russian Civil War and probably prevented the dismemberment of Russia. He prevented the dismemberment of Germany except for the Polish Corridor, which was deemed to be essential to the viability of the new Polish nation. He prevented the imposition of a truly Carthaginian peace on Germany. He created the League of Nations, which had all instrumentalities at hand necessary to prevent aggression in the future. The Second World War occurred, not because the instrument to prevent it did not exist, but because the leaders (and peoples) of Great Britain, France, and the United States lost their nerve and were unwilling to run the risks of stopping the Japanese, Mussolini, and Hitler when it would have been relatively easy to do so.

A third achievement was Wilson's strengthening of the principle of the peaceful settlement of international disputes and the avoidance of war if conceivably possible. Twice he personally prevented seemingly irresistible events from plunging the United States into war with Mexico. He fought long and hard to avoid participation in the World War. He endured egregious violations of American neutral rights and taunts by his enemies that he was a moral coward, afraid, rather than too proud, to fight. His success in maintaining American neutrality for two and a half years in these circumstances was no mean achievement in itself. He accepted belligerency in 1917 in order to hasten the end of the war and give him the opportunity to take leadership for peace and reconstruction of the world order.

His final achievement was to lay strong foundations for the tradition that the American people can best serve mankind by committing their resources and power to the quest for peace through international cooperation. It is almost trite to say that Wilson, by his fight for American membership in and leadership of the League of Nations, did more than any other single man in our history to build this tradition. The fact that he failed momentarily is of minor significance in the long sweep of history. The United Nations, the vindication of Wilson's vision, is still the best hope for peace, despite its failures and uncertain future.

This review of Wilson the diplomatist has necessarily been somewhat subjective. Opinions about Wilson will continue to vary. He was not a small man, and he still evokes strong reactions one way or the other. On one point, however, all historians would agree—that it made a great difference that he lived and played his part in world affairs. As Sir Winston Churchill once put it, "Writing with every sense of respect, it seems no exaggeration to pronounce that the action of the United States with its repercussions on the history of the world depended, during the awful period of Armageddon, upon the workings of this man's mind and spirit to the exclusion of almost every other factor; and that he played a part in the fate of nations incomparably more direct and personal than any other man."

2

Wilson and the Problems of Neutrality, 1914-1917

For Woodrow Wilson, who had a positive disinclination to play the game of power politics, events on the international stage intruded fatefully from 1914 to 1917. By the spring of 1915, the United States was the only great power not directly involved in the war then raging from Europe to the Far East. Wilson desired only to deal fairly with both sides, to avoid military involvement, and to bring the war to an end as rapidly as possible. Like Jefferson and Madison a century earlier, however, he soon discovered that neutrality has many perplexities and perils.

Wilson's responses to the challenges to America's peace and security raised by the death grapple of the opposing alliances is still often misunderstood, notwithstanding scores of books and articles. Historians and publicists have too often looked for culprits instead of facts. They have too often misunderstood the facts when they found them. They have too often written as if Wilson and his advisers made policies in a vacuum, independent of conflicting pressures. If we can see Wilson's policies during the period of neutrality in the light of his convictions and objectives, the events and pressures (both domestic and foreign) that constantly played upon him, and the options available to him, then we will see that his tasks in foreign policy at this most critical juncture in the twentieth century were neither simple nor easy.

The most significant pressures affecting Wilson's decisions throughout the period 1914 to 1917 were the attitudes and opinions of the American people toward the war and their country's proper relation to it. Few Presidents in American history have been more keenly aware of the risks that a political leader runs when he ceases to speak for the preponderant majority. "The ear of the leader must ring with the voices of the people. He cannot be of the school of the prophets; he must be of the number of those who studiously serve the slow-paced daily demand." Wilson had written this in his great essay "Leaders of Men" in 1890. He well remembered these words as he formulated his policies toward the belligerents in the First World War.

The dominant American sentiment from 1914 to 1917 can be summarily characterized by the single adjective "neutral." Americans, to be sure, had decided opinions and reactions. Probably, a substantial minority were sentimentally pro-Ally and reacted sharply to particular events like the German invasion of Belgium, the burning of Louvain, and the sinking of the *Lusitania.* On the other hand, the sizable German- and Irish-American populations tended to be strongly pro-German, as did many Jews on account of Russian membership in the Triple Entente. Nonetheless, however the scales of American public opinion tipped, the preponderant majority of Americans did not believe that their interests and security were vitally involved in the outcome of the war. They naturally desired to save their sons from the ghastly carnage on the western front. The prevalence and stubborn force of neutralism, in spite of severe provocations and all the efforts of propagandists on both sides, was at one and the same time the unifying force in American politics and the compelling reality that Wilson had to face from 1914 to 1917.

Yet it would be a serious error to conclude from the foregoing that Wilson was a prisoner of public opinion, and that his will to adopt stern measures was paralyzed by the counterforce of neutralism. The evidence points overwhelmingly to the conclusion that Wilson himself was substantially neutral in attitude. While recognizing the constraints that public opinion put upon him, he acted during all periods of crisis from his "lonely eminence of power" on a basis of what he thought was right. Above all, he believed that the United States could best serve mankind by doing everything possible to bring the war to a speedy end. As he wrote to a friend during the submarine crisis of 1915, it would be the greatest calamity possible if the United States become involved in the war, because belligerency would end all chances for American mediation. His one great objective from 1914 to 1917 was peace; every policy that he executed during this period has to be understood within the framework of this overriding goal.

Never once during the period of neutrality did Wilson explain orally or set down in writing all his personal views about the causes of the war. However, there is a good deal of indirect evidence about his thinking on this subject. He believed that the causes of the war were deep-rooted and complex—growing militarism on the Continent, the divisive nationalisms of the Austro-Hungarian Empire, Russia's drive for access to the Mediterranean, Germany's seizure of Alsace-Lorraine in 1871, the German challenge to Britain's naval and commercial supremacy, the system of rival alliances that had been formed after the Franco-Prussian War, and, in general, the imperialistic rivalries of the late nineteenth and early twentieth centuries. As he put it to Walter Page in 1916, England owned the world, and Germany wanted it too. That Wilson believed that these were the root causes of the war is indicated by the fact that he singled them out as the prime causes of international conflict and the ones that would have to be removed if the world was ever to enjoy lasting peace.

It followed, therefore, that all the belligerents were to some degree responsible for the war. Nor was Wilson naive about conflicting war objectives. To him it was clear that all the belligerents sincerely believed that they were fighting for their existence, but that they all wanted a smashing victory in order to increase their power, win new territory, and impose crushing indemnities upon their enemies. Such a settlement, he was convinced, would inevitably generate another war within the near future. Hence Wilson believed that the best settlement would be a stalemate ending in a peace settlement based largely upon the *status quo ante bellum.*

He stated his deep convictions with prophetic accuracy in a speech or a draft of a peace note that he dictated to his stenographer in the autumn of 1916. He did not deliver the speech or send the note because he realized that he could not say such things publicly. It is printed here for the first time in full, in spite of its length, because it reveals, better than any other document, his understanding of the nature of modern total war and of the dire consequences of total victory.

When the air is burdened with peace rumors and the diplomatic wires which girdle the world are hot with overtures and suggestions of peace, it is a pertinent question to ask, What are the terms of a lasting peace? For, with the horrible nightmare still upon it, the world will listen to no suggestion which does not seek to safeguard it against such a recurrence in the future. When this unprecedented eruption subsides, if we are still to live over the volcano, we must know that the last spark of life in it is extinguished. War, before this one, used to be a sort of national excursion, a necessary holiday to vary the monotony of a lazy, tranquil existence on which the population turned out to celebrate their freedom from conventional restraint, with brilliant battles lost and won, national heroes decorated, and all sharing in the glory accruing to the state. But can this vast, gruesome contest of systematized destruction which we have witnessed for the last two years be pictured in that light, in which all the great nations of Europe were involved, wherein no brilliant battles such as we thrill to read about were either lost or won, but few national figures decorated above the rest, and no particular glory accrued to any state; wherein the big, striking thing for the imagination to respond to was the untold human suffering?

In assessing the terms of a lasting peace, we are too apt to allow our sympathies with one side or the other to override our judgment. If we are pro-Ally, German militarism must first be crushed ere a lasting peace is tenable. If our sympathies are the other way, then the first essential to a lasting peace is the defeat of British navalism. Both contentions, it must be admitted, are sound, convincing arguments, not only to their respective authors, but to the unprejudiced neutral who has no interest in the war except to bring it to an end. In the extreme point to which Germany has carried its military organization, he sees a serious menace to the permanent peace of Europe and of the world. But in no less a degree does he recognize the source of international friction existent in the absolute control of the seas by Great Britain, or any other one power. There are other objects to be attained, however, which the partisan does not usually consider in his assessment of the case.

Assuming that German militarism were crushed by the decisive defeat of German arms, would that be the prelude to a lasting peace? Is it necessary to answer the question? Would the breaking of British navalism bring it on? It is only necessary to go back to the war of 1870 to disprove either assumption. With France then hopelessly beaten, a huge indemnity levied upon her, and two of her fairest provinces torn from her bosom, it was thought that, thus crippled, she would reconcile herself to the superiority of German arms and in time forget the ravishment of her territory. On the contrary, then was born one of the germs of the present war: she paid the indemnity and reconstructed her whole life, with the single object of excelling German military organization and regaining Alsace and Lorraine.

On the other hand, Germany, flushed with victory and puffed up at the ease with which it had broken the vaunted military power of France, began to dream greater dreams of conquest and power. Another germ was hatched which was to develop into the dreadful malady of the present conflict. We see it abundantly demonstrated in the pages of history that the decisive victories and defeats of wars are seldom the conclusive ones. One Sedan brings on another, and victory is an intoxicant that fires the national brain and leaves a craving for more.

Were Germany, by a decisive victory, to bring her enemies to their knees, the partitioning of territory would at once be begun and a huge indemnity levied to stand her cost of the war; and from that minute on she would have to prepare herself for another conflict which would inevitably come. Even she, with her unmatched genius for military organization, could never hope to keep the whole of Europe in military subjection. With the defeat of Germany, the inevitable procedure would be the annexing of her colonies, the allotting out of the territory of her allies, and an indemnity collected for the rehabilitation of Belgium, Serbia, and Rumania; perhaps, too, for the reimbursement in part of the military expenses of the Entente. Needless to say, such an outrage to her pride would never be forgotten; it would rankle in her breast as did the rape of Alsace-Lorraine to the French. Based on either of these hypotheses, an enduring peace is the empty talk of partisan dreamers.

25

The crowned victor in a mighty conflict too easily forgets the suffering and the agony endured in achieving the end. The memory of the death struggle which all but overpowered it is dimmed by the growing sun of glory and is finally eclipsed altogether. In the language of the street, the victorious nation, as the man, gets "cocky" again, places another chip on its shoulder and becomes unendurable as a neighbor. As a consequence, it has another fight on its hands ere its sword grows rusty.

What, then, are the terms which make for an enduring peace? The present war, with its unprecedented human waste and suffering and its drain of material resource, presents an unparalleled opportunity for the statesmen of the world to make such a peace possible. Never before in the world's history have two great armies been in effect so equally matched; never before have the losses and the slaughter been so great with as little gain in military advantage. Both sides have grown weary of the apparently hopeless task of bringing the conflict to an end by the force of arms; inevitably they are being forced to the realization that it can only be brought about by the attrition of human suffering, in which the victor suffers hardly less than the vanquished. This may require one year, maybe two.

To bring about a peace with these circumstances prevailing, when the big, understanding thing to be remembered by all nations was the uselessness of the utter sacrifices made, would be to give it the essential basis of endurance—the psychological basis. Deprived of glory, war loses all its charm; when the only attribute of it is suffering, then it is something to be detested. In the revelation of the modern processes of battle, it has already lost some of its halo. The mechanical game of slaughter of today has not the same fascination as the zest of intimate combat of former days; and trench warfare and poisonous gases are elements which detract alike from the excitement and the tolerance of modern conflict. With maneuver almost a thing of the past, any given point can admittedly be carried by the sacrifice of enough men and ammunition. Where is any longer the glory commensurate with the sacrifice of the millions of men required in modern warfare to carry and defend Verdun? With this experience conducing, the aim of far-sighted statesmen should be to make of this mightiest of conflicts an object lesson for the future by bringing it to a close with the objects of each group of belligerents still unaccomplished and all the magnificent sacrifices on both sides gone for naught. Only then would war be eliminated as in a way to being a means of attaining national ambitions. The world would be free to build its new peace structure on the solidest foundation it has ever possessed.

In the event of such a peace, the objects for which all the belligerents are fighting will be entrusted for accomplishment to the convention which is to assemble after the war, as should be.

About the relative merits of the causes of the Allies and the Central Powers, Wilson said little during the period 1914–1917. During the first months of the war, when it seemed that the Germans might win on the western front, he was emotionally pro-British. For example, at the height of the first Battle of the Marne, he told the British Ambassador in Washington, Sir Cecil Spring Rice, that everything that the United States stood for depended upon the outcome of that battle. Several times later, he avowed his personal sympathy for the Allied cause to close friends. However, this ardor cooled perceptibly once it became apparent that the Allies were fighting for conquest; certainly by the autumn of 1916 Wilson was as neutral in thought as it was possible for any American to have been. Meanwhile, as he said and wrote several times to high German officials, he had great admiration for the German people and their remarkable achievements, did not want to see Germany crushed, and desired to see German power in Europe maintained as a stabilizing and balancing force.

Wilson, fortified by these convictions, struggled hard, and on the whole successfully, to be impartial in "thought as well as in deed." He had a remarkable capacity to subordinate his personal feelings and emotions to his rational processes and to act upon what he thought were right convictions and principles. He sealed himself off from the passionate arguments of partisans by simply refusing to listen to them. "I recall," Lansing later wrote in his diary, "that ... his attitude toward evidence of German atrocities in Belgium and toward accounts of the horrors of submarine warfare ... [was that] he would not read of them and showed anger if the details were called to his attention."

Since American sentiment was against involvement, a policy of strict official neutrality was the only possible course for the United States government in 1914. This fact prompted Wilson's official proclamations of neutrality, supplemented by his appeal to the American people to be impartial in thought as well as in deed; the subsequent definition by the State Department of the elaborate technical rules of neutrality; and the establishment of a Joint State and Navy Neutrality Board to advise the various departments of the government upon the correct interpretation of international law.

The records that reveal the formulation of these policies of neutrality furnish convincing evidence that their authors were both resolute and high-minded in their determination to be fair to both sides. Indeed, Wilson and Bryan (the man who chiefly influenced him in formulating the rules of neutrality) were so intent upon being fair to the Germans that they executed policies during the first months of the war that were decidedly disadvantageous to the Allies, if not actually unneutral. One was to prevent the sale of submarine parts, and hence parts of any naval vessels, by a private American firm to the British government on the ground that such sale would be "contrary to . . . strict neutrality." This policy was adopted in spite of advice from Counselor Robert Lansing and the Joint Neutrality Board to the effect that the ban on the sale of submarine parts was contrary to accepted international law.

Much more damaging to the Allies was the administration's second effort to lean over backward—the ban on loans by private American bankers to the belligerent governments, which Wilson permitted Bryan to impose on the sentimental ground that money was "the worst of all contrabands—it commands all other things." There were good domestic reasons for a *temporary* ban. International markets were in chaos at the outbreak of the war, and the administration was trying to stem the flow of gold to Europe. However, the ban on loans was unneutral, as we will see in later pages. It was highly prejudicial to the Allies because it denied them the right to finance their purchases in the American market.

In addition, Wilson personally sponsored two measures highly disadvantageous to the Allies and unneutral in spirit if not in fact. One was a change in the ship registry law, put into effect by an act approved on August 18, 1914, which made it easy for German and other foreign shipping firms to take out American registry. The other was a plan to establish a federal corporation to purchase ships, including German ships in American ports, to carry exports to Europe, including, presumably, noncontraband (goods, etc., destined for civilians) to Germany. This, the so-called ship purchase bill, failed to pass in March 1915 only because of a determined filibuster by senators who said that it was unneutral and would involve the United States in grave controversies with the Allies.

The British Foreign Secretary, Sir Edward Grey, complained bitterly that these measures were unneutral and reflected the anti-British sentiment of the Washington government. This was decidedly untrue. Wilson was only trying to obtain desperately needed shipping. He and Bryan did not realize the long-term consequences of the ban on loans. When the rules were clear-cut, they were resolute in abiding by international law. For example, Wilson and Bryan stoutly resisted a German-American move in Congress in late 1914 and early 1915 for an embargo on the export of munitions.

The acid tests of Wilson's neutrality were his policies toward Great Britain from 1914 to 1917. He has been condemned by the so-called revisionist historians for becoming the captive of pro-Allied influences among his advisers, particularly Colonel House; for condoning such sweeping British control of neutral commerce that the Germans had no choice by 1917 but to resort to a desperate counter-measure—all-out submarine warfare against *all* commerce; and for permitting American prosperity, even well-being, to become dependent upon exports and loans to the Allies. The revisionists (and others) have condemned Wilson, above all, for permitting a state of affairs to develop that made it inevitable that the United States would go to war if the success of the Allied cause was ever seriously threatened.

Like most fallacious arguments, this one has an appearance of cogency. Wilson did accept far-reaching British measures of maritime warfare. American neutrality worked greatly to the advantage of the Allies and equally greatly to the disadvantage of Germany. The fallacy lies in the implication that Wilson wanted this situation to develop, contributed significantly to its development, and could have prevented it.

29

One scholar has argued recently that Wilson's single most important decision was to permit Americans to trade with the Allies, because the war trade soon interlocked the Anglo-American economies and eventually led the Germans to conclude that the United States could do less damage to them as a belligerent than as a neutral. There are three fallacies in this argument. First, Americans were free under the laws of the United States to sell to whom they pleased. Wilson had no statutory authority whatsoever to stop *any* transatlantic trade. Actually, no one in Washington made any decision for or against trade, or even thought about making one. Second, a neutral had obligations as well as rights under international law as it was codified in 1914. One of these obligations was to permit its citizens to trade with any and all belligerents. But more about this later. Third, Wilson could never have received authority from Congress to stop exports, even the exports of war material, unless he had been able to convince Congress and the country that an embargo was necessary to protect American security or promote some overriding national goal like peace.

Anglo-American relations developed *in stages* in response to particular pressures, events, and forces. The first stage, lasting during the first year of the war, was perhaps the most critical because it was the time when Wilson and his advisers worked out their basic response to the British maritime system. That response was in turn largely governed by two domestic realities: the overwhelming and virtually unanimous desire of the American people to be neutral, and pressures from American producers and exporters for uninhibited trade in noncontraband with the Central Powers.

In response, Wilson worked hard during the early months of the war to keep the channels of international commerce open. First, he proposed the adoption of a code, which, if accepted, would have severely weakened the British system of maritime warfare. Specifically, Wilson, on August 6, 1914, proposed that all belligerents adopt the rules of naval warfare laid down in the Declaration of London of 1909 (a treaty that Great Britain and the United States had never ratified). It permitted free transit for most goods except those that were clearly absolute contraband, that is, goods obviously destined for armed forces. When the British rejected this proposal, Wilson came back on October 16, 1914 with a compromise that would still have seriously constrained British sea power. Once again, the British refused. Wilson then announced that the United States would assert and defend all its rights under international law and treaties.

However, in seeking to defend these rights, Wilson ran head-on into a reality more intractable than the reality of domestic pressures —British determination to use sea power to prevent American ships and goods from going to the sustenance of the German war economy and military forces.

British control of the seas washing the shores of western Europe began with relatively mild measures (for example, during the first eight months of the war the British permitted the export of food and raw materials like cotton to Germany) and culminated in the suppression of all commerce to the Central Powers in March 1915. For the British, this was not a matter of adhering to the rules of international law or of violating them: It was a matter of achieving the supreme British objective—depriving the Central Powers of vital goods and raw materials. But the British were keenly aware that it was necessary that they achieve this goal without going past the point of no return in their relations with the United States. Sir Edward Grey stated the matter frankly in his memoirs:

> Blockade of Germany was essential to the victory of the Allies, but the ill-will of the United States meant their certain defeat. . . . It was better therefore to carry on the war without blockade, if need be, than to incur a break with the United States about contraband and thereby deprive the Allies of the resources necessary to carry on the war at all or with any chance of success. The object of diplomacy, therefore, was to secure the maximum of blockade that could be enforced without a rupture with the United States.

The crucial question all along, therefore, was whether the United States—the only neutral power strong enough effectively to challenge the British measures—would acquiesce or resist to the point of threatening to use force. The American response during this formative period was, in brief, to accept the British system, maintain strong and steady pressure upon London in particular shipping cases, and reserve all American rights for future adjudication. In the circumstances, this response was inevitable. Only an administration that desired Germany's triumph and had Congress and the country behind it in such a desire could have responded differently.

The British maritime system, in spite of American allegations to the contrary, was on the whole legitimate and legal, by traditional customs and practices. It was legitimate rather than fraudulent, and legal rather than capricious and terroristic (like the German submarine campaign in 1915), because the British did effectively and easily command the seas. Thus they were able to execute their maritime controls in an orderly fashion and without any threat to human life. Overwhelming command of the seas gave much validity to the British long-range blockade of Germany by a moving cordon of cruisers. The argument that the British should use methods required in the days of the sailing ship (such as the rule that blockades had to be offshore in order to be legal) did not have much cogency in the changed circumstances of the twentieth century, that is, after the introduction of submarines and floating mines.

Moreover, the British were wise and shrewd in establishing and carrying out their maritime system. American reaction would undoubtedly have been violent had the British instituted a total long-range blockade of Germany at the beginning of the war. Instead, the British expanded their controls gradually with a careful eye upon American public opinion. Moreover, they shrewdly used the opportunities provided by severe crises in German-American relations to institute their harshest measures.

The British also took great care never to offend so many American interests at one time that retaliation would have been inevitable, or any single interest group powerful enough by itself to compel retaliation. Southern cotton growers, with their strong representation in a Democratic Congress, constituted that single interest group. The disorganization of international markets and exchange following the outbreak of the war temporarily severely depressed the price of cotton and set off a panic in the South. The British government did not declare cotton contraband; on the contrary, it gave public assurances that it would not prevent the shipment of cotton to the Central

Powers. Even so, the British (and the French even more so) were determined to prevent cotton from going to Germany because it was an ingredient of gunpowder and essential to the clothing of the German army. Thus the British put cotton on the list of absolute contraband in August 1915. At the same time, they underwrote the entire American cotton market by buying enough cotton to maintain the price at its level of 1913. By so doing, they averted what might have been an irresistible southern pressure in Congress for retaliation. In addition, the British, although ruthless in enforcing their blockade, were careful to avoid significant injury to American exporters. They *confiscated* only the most obvious absolute contraband; in all doubtful cases (like food products and meat) they paid full value for cargoes seized. The chief British objective was to control and benefit from, not to destroy, American commerce.

The British Foreign Office was also extremely adept in using language and symbolism to justify the measures being executed by the Admiralty and the Ministry of Blockade. The Foreign Office justified the British martime system in 1914 by appealing to international law and the American sense of fair play; moreover, it made an honest effort when possible to meet American objections halfway. When the British instituted a total blockade of the Central Powers in March 1915, they invoked the ancient right of retaliation (against a German declaration of a submarine "blockade"). Thus the British succeeded (before the summer of 1916) in giving a *legal* character to the issues in controversy with the United States; they also avoided seeming to challenge American sovereignty and inherent national rights. In short, they were careful not to wound American national pride and dignity, as they had done by impressment and egregious violations of American trading rights before the War of 1812. Consequently, the Washington government had to reply in the same *legal* language that the British used. Moreover, the British were extremely lucky to have Grey, who was extremely sensitive to American opinions and feelings, as Foreign Secretary at the outbreak of the war.

Finally, the British pointed with considerable cogency to precedents established by the American government itself during the Civil War to justify their own blockade measures as legitimate adaptations to a changed technology. To be sure, the British drew some inaccurate analogies. Still, on the whole, the American government found itself hoisted on its own petard by its maritime practices from 1861 to 1865. As the late Samuel Flagg Bemis once put it, the legal issues between the British and American governments from 1914 to 1917 were really mute.

Wilson's decision not to attempt to break the British blockade was inevitable in view of the foregoing facts and considerations, *if his objective was to maintain as best he could the neutrality of the United States.* An absolute neutrality was impossible in practice because of the total character of the war and the importance of the United States in the world economy. Any action by the United States was bound to confer a benefit upon one side and an injury on the other, at least indirectly. In these circumstances, neutrality consisted of doing the things that would give the least unwarranted or the smallest advantage to one side or the other. By this standard it would have been more unneutral than neutral for Wilson to have broken the British blockade by vindicating rights that were highly dubious under international law and American practices.

From the standpoint of practical and realistic considerations, Wilson's *de facto* acceptance of the British maritime system was wise. One result of destroying the British blockade would have been the wrecking of the friendship between the United States and the only other important democracies in the world, Great Britain and France. The other result would have been the probable victory of Germany, which by 1917 was implacably, if understandably, hostile to the United States. In short, destroying the British blockade would have brought not a single compensating gain to the United States while it would, at the same time, have imperiled its own national security. Only the achievement of some great political objective, like a secure peace settlement (not winning commercial advantages or vindicating dubious neutral rights), would have justified Wilson in undertaking a determined challenge to British sea power.

The second stage in Anglo-American relations lasted from the summer of 1915 to the late spring of 1916 and saw the development of the natural economic consequences of the American acceptance of tightening British control of the seas. One consequence was the burgeoning of exports from the United States to the Allies as the former became the storehouse and armory of the latter. A second consequence was the increase of power that the Washington government could exercise politically over the Allies. But more about this in its proper context.

This situation did not of course occur all at once. Bryan's ban on loans of 1914 had been motivated in part by a desire to prevent the outflow of American gold during a time when American bankers were having great difficulty in meeting their international obligations. The shoe was on the other foot by the summer of 1915; the British government, while not yet in dire straits, was having difficulty maintaining the pound. Actually, Bryan had taken the lead in reversing his own policy by quietly approving a $50 million "credit" by J. P. Morgan and Company to the French government in March 1915. However, the issue of the administration's attitude toward loans to the belligerents was forced into the open in the late summer of 1915. Then the British and French governments decided to float a $500 million public loan (that is, one intended for sale to private investors) in the United States, and the Morgans formed a nationwide banking syndicate to underwrite and sell the Anglo-French bonds.

Bryan's ban, or what remained of it, could not have survived the large-scale development of the war trade because, in the first place, it was potentially nearly as disastrous to the United States as to the Allies. American material well-being had always depended upon world trade; in 1915 it depended upon trade with the Allied world. It was impossible for the ban to survive, in the second place, because it was an unneutral policy that threatened the growth, even the continuation, of the chief economic consequence of American neutrality —the legitimate war trade. Wilson and his advisers were all well aware of these facts. Wilson decided that the correct policy was for the United States government neither to approve nor disapprove of the Anglo-French loan, any more than it had approved or disapproved of the war trade.

It was a logical and neutral decision. It also enhanced the security of the United States. Britain's existence depended upon her ability to command the seas and keep open the channels of overseas trade and credit. The sale of goods and extension of credits by private parties to belligerents were neutral in law, tradition, and practice.

Unwarranted interference with such intercourse would have gravely penalized British sea power to the great advantage of German power on the land. American security probably depended upon the continuation of British sea power. It is unquestionable that the Allied war effort would eventually (by the spring of 1917) have ground to a halt without American credit. Therefore, the effect of a continuation of the credit embargo would most likely have been German victory in Europe, with serious portents for the security of the United States. At the least, Americans would have lived in a dangerous world if they had had to deal with a militaristic and imperialistic Germany—triumphant, strident, and in effective control of Europe from the English Channel to the Urals.

The second stage in Anglo-American relations also witnessed the apparent congruence of the diplomatic policies of the two countries on Wilson's overriding objective—peace. During the autumn of 1915, Colonel House devised a plan by which the American and British leaders would join hands to press for an end of the war through Wilson's mediation. Sir Edward Grey replied that his government would cooperate only if the Washington administration would also promise to join a postwar international organization to achieve disarmament on land, guarantee the freedom of the seas, and preserve peace through united action against aggressors. Wilson consented and, with great hope and expectations, sent House to London, Paris, and Berlin in January 1916.

House worked out the terms of a plan with Grey on February 22, 1916. This document, known as the House-Grey Memorandum, stipulated that Wilson, upon hearing from England and France that the time was ripe, should call a conference to end the war. If the Allies accepted the invitation and Germany refused it, the United States would "probably" enter the war on the side of the Allies. Should the conference meet and Germany refused to agree to a "reasonable" settlement, then the United States would also "probably" enter the war on the Allied side. Wilson approved the plan at once after inserting the "probablys."

The revisionists have pointed to the House-Grey Memorandum as conclusive proof that Wilson had abandoned neutrality and intended to take the country into the war at the first opportunity.

There can now be little doubt that House conceived of the memorandum as an instrument of intervention. He was convinced that the Germans would resort to all-out submarine warfare and drive the United States into war in the near future. In this case, the United States would be fighting merely in defense of national rights and honor. He wanted to use American belligerency for a larger and nobler purpose—the establishment of a secure and lasting peace.

Wilson shared House's desire for a just and lasting settlement. However, he conceived of the House-Grey Memorandum as the instrument by which he could achieve his two main objectives—to avert American involvement by bringing the war to an end, and to establish a lasting peace. It seemed that the best, indeed the only, hope for peace at this time lay in Anglo-American cooperation. Wilson certainly relized that the House-Grey plan carried some risks. It was necessary to give positive assurances to the Allies. They would have been at a fatal disadvantage in a peace conference without American support since Germany occupied a third of France and part of Russia. There was, moveover, the risk of war with Germany if it refused to approve an armistice or proved to be unreasonable at a peace conference if one met. However, Wilson was certain that no government would be able to rally its people for a resumption of the fighting once it had ended. Thus he gave the necessary assurances in the belief that the risk of American belligerency was insignificant as compared to the dangers of war with Germany if he did not bring the war to an end.

In the final analysis, Wilson's willingness to accept the risk of war must be judged by the kind of peace settlement that he wanted to achieve through the instrumentality of the House-Grey Memorandum. To him, a "reasonable" settlement meant a return to the *status quo ante bellum,* with only minor adjustments and with no annexations and indemnities. It meant, above all, a new world order with guarantees for the peace and security of all nations. Colonel House, in his final discussions with the British leaders, made it crystal clear that this, and this only, was the kind of settlement that Wilson was willing to use the House-Grey plan to achieve. As House told his conferees in London, Wilson would "throw the weight of the United States on the side of those wanting a just settlement—a settlement which would make another such war impossible." We will come back to the House-Grey Memorandum and its fate in the next chapter. Let us now turn to German-American relations during the period we have just discussed.

So long as the British controlled the seas and the Germans commanded the strategic territories and resources of Europe, Wilson's task was the relatively easy one of accepting a *de facto* situation and of pursuing the most impartial policies within this balance of power. Thus he made no official comment on the German invasion of Belgium and other gross German violations of international law and the laws of humanity. In like manner, he accepted the British maritime system. In this situation of stalemate there was little likelihood of an Anglo-American rupture and no possibility of serious German-American conflict.

However, the German decision in early 1915 to try to break the stalemate by using submarines against maritime commerce created a potentially perilous situation for the United States because the submarine war could raise an issue of fundamental rights to the United States—the safety of its ships and the security of its citizens against wanton murder on the high seas. Before we see how Wilson met the challenge of the submarine, let us consider the motivation of the German leaders and some larger aspects of the questions raised by the use of submarines against merchant shipping.

First, German leaders made their decisions regarding the use of the submarine entirely upon a basis of what they thought were objective calculations and Germany's self-interest, for example, the number and capacities of available submarines, and the military situation in Europe and the impact of American intervention in case of an all-out underseas campaign. The Germans did offer to abandon their ruthless submarine campaign if the Allies would adopt the Declaration of London as the rules governing maritime warfare. Wilson persuaded the British to permit free transit of food to Germany in return for German abandonment of the ruthless submarine war and the use of poisonous gases. But the Germans demanded nothing less than free transit of vital raw materials, and the British naturally refused to give up their most effective economic weapon. Only Wilson could have forced the British to yield any significant concessions. He was prepared to take some such action, but only for a price—German cooperation in reestablishing international law on the seas as a preliminary to peace. However, Wilson was not willing to be a cat's-paw of German diplomacy. The chief, and, in the final showdown, the only reason that the Germans used the submarine was to cut off Britain from her life-giving sources of supply and thereby to win the war. The Germans would have used the submarine to knock England out of the war when they had enough U-boats to accomplish this goal even if the British had long since given up their blockade altogether. In short, calculations of military advantage dictated the German prosecution of the submarine campaign.

Second, since the submarine was in 1915 a new weapon of naval warfare, there was no special international law to govern its use. The only laws applicable were what were called the rules of cruiser warfare. They required warships to warn merchant ships before sinking them or taking them as prizes, and to make provisions for the safety of crews and passengers. Everyone assumed at first that it was impossible for submarines to observe these rules on account of their frailty, small size, and susceptibility to ramming. Eventually, however, the Germans were able to conduct a successful cruiser-type submarine war, even against armed ships, as we will see.

Third, the submarine blockade, when it was inaugurated in February 1915, was a fraud and sham, since the Germans were then able to keep at most only seven U-boats at one time in all the waters surrounding the British Isles. In fact, the Germans launched the "blockade" with four submarines in service in that area. A year later, the German Admiralty could send only eleven or twelve submarines into western waters at one time. Moreover, in the beginning at least, the submarine campaign was primarily a terroristic weapon intended to frighten neutral shipping and enhance German morale. For example, the German people hailed the sinking of large British passenger liners as great blows against British sea power; militarily, they were insignificant.

Fourth, while Anglo-American disputes over trading rights involved only property interests, the German submarine war raised an issue that no great power could evade or arbitrate—the safety of its citizens in pursuits and areas where they had an undoubted right to be. It is inconceivable that Wilson could have thought of going to war with the British over issues of search and seizure or of blockade. It is equally inconceivable that he would not have been willing to think about going to war with a government that instructed its naval commanders wantonly to slaughter American citizens on the high seas.

Earlier writers have said that Wilson had one policy toward the submarine campaign—implacable opposition to it. This is egregiously wrong. Actually, Wilson followed a number of policies in response to the changing circumstances of the U-boat campaign and also in response to his own larger diplomatic objectives.

He announced his first policy in a note to Germany on February 10, 1915, soon after the German proclamation of the submarine "blockade." Wilson simply, but clearly, affirmed the right of American vessels to use the seas subject to the limitations permitted by international law. He warned that the United States would hold Germany to "strict accountability" (a conventional diplomatic term) for *American* ships and lives lost on account of illegal submarine attacks. Wilson's wording was deliberately vague about the security of Americans on *belligerent* ships. It was the only position that Wilson could have taken without abandoning national rights and dignity so ignominiously as to lose all power for good in the world. Actually, the Germans soon gave sweeping guarantees regarding American ships. This was never a point of serious conflict between the United States and Germany before 1917.

The issue of the security of Americans on belligerent ships soon arose. However, it involved only the right of American citizens to travel on *passenger* ships under conditions of safety specified by international law. A German submarine sank without warning a British liner, *Falaba,* on March 28, 1915; one American was lost, and Wilson's advisers in the State Department squared off in a momentous debate over a proper response. One group, led by Bryan, argued that American rights were not sufficiently involved to warrant a protest against submarine attacks against Allied ships when Americans were traveling on them. Bryan also pleaded that the spirit of neutrality demanded that the United States acquiesce in German violations of international law and agree to postpone their arbitration until after the war, just as it had done in cases of British violations. The other group, headed by Lansing, replied that the killing of the American citizen had been a flagrant violation of international law and American rights, and that the United States had to make peremptory demands in order to defend its rights and honor.

Wilson had no desire to become caught in the cross fire while the two giants fought it out on the seas. He agreed with Lansing that an American citizen had been wantonly killed. However, he was strongly moved by Bryan's arguments. In the end, he decided to make no protest at all. This is undoubtedly the course that he would have followed in the future if the Germans had confined their attacks to Allied cargo ships and indicated any concern at all for the safety of American citizens on passenger ships.

This policy of evasion soon became impossible. On May 7, 1915, a German U-boat sank the large unarmed British liner *Lusitania* without warning in the Irish Sea, with the loss of about 1,200 persons —men, women, and children—including 128 Americans. Wilson had to respond, so dramatic was the incident, so atrocious was the deed in the eyes of the American people, so flagrant was the violation of elementary national rights.

Legally, Wilson would have been justified in making a peremptory demand; but, as he told his stenographer, he would not be stampeded into war. From May to July he pounded out, on his own typewriter, notes to the German government. First, he appealed on high humanitarian grounds to the German authorities to abandon the submarine campaign altogether and to join hands with him in trying to establish genuine freedom of the seas. The Germans refused. Then, in secret messages to the Imperial German Chancellor, Theobald von Bethmann Hollweg, and in a second public note, Wilson narrowed the issues in dispute to the safety of life upon *unarmed* passenger liners; he also again appealed for German cooperation in a campaign to restore the freedom of the seas, adding that he was prepared "to carry this thing through with the British to the end." Again, the Germans were unresponsive (Bethmann Hollweg did not even answer Wilson's messages). In a third note, Wilson said that recent events had demonstrated that it was possible to conduct a cruiser-type submarine campaign; in other words, he accepted the legality of the use of submarines against merchant shipping under certain conditions. But he also said that the United States would regard the unwarned sinking of an

41

unarmed passenger ship as a "deliberately unfriendly" act, that is, as a cause for severing diplomatic relations with the German Empire, and perhaps for war.

The issue came to a head when a German submarine sank another large British liner, *Arabic,* with the loss of two American lives, on August 19, 1915. This time Wilson did not write notes, but he made it clear to the German government through its Ambassador in Washington, Count Johann Heinrich von Bernstorff, that he would break diplomatic relations if the Berlin government did not yield to his earlier demand. At the same time, as he wrote to Edith Bolling Galt, he was determined not to go to war if the Germans did not yield. Instead, he said, he planned to break relations with Germany and then call a conference of the neutral nations for the purpose of establishing real freedom of the seas, and he meant to be as hard on one side as on the other. (The neutrals, with the United States at their head, would do this by boycotting all trade with the side that refused to observe international law.)

The German leaders finally came to their senses and promised, in the so-called *Arabic* pledge of September 1, 1915, not to sink passenger liners without warning and providing for the safety of passengers and crews. There followed a second crisis over disavowal of the sinking of the *Arabic.* The German Ambassador solved this crisis by giving a formal disavowal on his own authority. The German government then disavowed the Ambassador's disavowal, but in such an ambiguous way that no one in Washington knew that the retraction had been made. Meanwhile, the German Emperor, William II, had called off the submarine campaign in British waters in order to make certain that no further *Lusitania* and *Arabic* incidents could occur.

The submarine issue was dormant until late December 1915. Then, relations between the United States and Germany became strained once again when Wilson and Lansing (now Secretary of State) began to press the Berlin authorities for a final settlement of the *Lusitania* case and demanded acknowledgment of the illegality of the sinking of the ship. The atmosphere was tense for a time, and there was talk of a break in relations. But in the end Wilson agreed to accept an apology and offer of payment of damages without an explicit

German admission of illegality. For one thing, Wilson did not want to endanger the peace by severing relations over what was rapidly becoming a stale case. More important, Wilson heeded House's advice that it would be unwise to imperil the chances of a peace conference at the very time when House seemed to be successfully negotiating for one.

Before the German and American governments could exchange notes closing the *Lusitania* case, a new controversy over armed ships exploded at the end of the *Lusitania* negotiations. The Allies had begun to arm merchant and passenger ships in the late summer of 1915. Wilson and Lansing agreed that it was unfair to expect a submarine to stop and warn a vessel that was capable of destroying it. Therefore, Lansing (with Wilson's approval) proposed to the Allied governments on January 18, 1916, a *modus vivendi* between the Allies and the Central Powers. The Allies would disarm their merchant ships in return for a German promise that submarines would follow the rules of visit and search before attacking them. If the Allies did not agree, Lansing warned, the United States might treat armed merchantmen as warships, thus barring them from American ports. It was a tremendous blunder. As Sir Edward Grey rightly said, the United States government was proposing a method for the systematic destruction of the British merchang marine. The British leaders also believed that Lansing's *modus vivendi,* along with the seemingly successful outcome of the *Lusitania* negotiations, marked Wilson's decision to come to terms with Germany—and all at Britain's expense!

Lansing informed the Austrian Chargé d'Affaires in Washington about the proposed *modus vivendi* on January 26. The Chargé said that the German and Austrian governments were contemplating declaring armed ships fair game for submarines. Lansing replied that "the sooner it was done the better." Seizing the opportunity, the German authorities announced on February 10, 1916, that submarines would attack *armed* enemy merchantmen without warning beginning February 29.

The fat was now very much in the fire. House, in urgent telegrams from London, pointed out that the mere suggestion of the *modus vivendi* had already raised doubts in British circles about Wilson's neutrality. Insistence on the *modus vivendi,* he added, would assuredly disqualify the President as a mediator insofar as the Allies were concerned. Wilson at once publicly jettisoned the *modus vivendi* and announced that he would defend the right of Americans to travel on armed ships if the Allies vetoed Lansing's proposal. He also headed off a rebellion in Congress by demanding and winning the defeat of resolutions in both houses (the Gore-McLemore resolutions) warning Americans not to travel on armed ships.

Actually, Wilson had no intention of going to war over armed ships. He was simply doing what he thought necessary to restore British confidence in him and to assure the success of the House-Grey plan. Ironically, in light of all that has been written about the armed ship controversy, it had no deleterious impact on German-American relations because Lansing, with Wilson's approval, soon imposed such severe limitations on the arming of merchantmen and laid down such stern rules against their offensive behavior that armed ships were helpless in defending themselves against submarines. Later, in early January 1917, the German government announced that submarines would sink armed merchantmen without warning. This time, Wilson let the announcement pass without public notice and told Lansing that he had no intention of risking war over armed ships. Meanwhile, the issue had never been a matter of controversy between the American and German governments.

The submarine issue came to a new head and, temporarily, to definitive resolution during the spring of 1916, when the German Admiralty unleashed its U-boats in what appeared to be an all-out campaign of terror around the British Isles. A submarine torpedoed the Channel packet *Sussex* on March 24, 1916, with eighty casualties; four American citizens were injured. Lansing, now obviously eager for war, advised an immediate severance of diplomatic relations. After long and tedious exchanges with Berlin, Wilson determined to force the issue once for all. On April 19, he went before Congress and read the note that he had just dispatched to Berlin. It ended with an ultimatum: "Unless the Imperial Government should now immediately declare and effect an abandonment of its present methods of submarine warfare against passenger and freight-carrying vessels, the Government of the United States can have no choice but to sever diplomatic relations with the German Empire altogether."

Wilson deliberately left it ambiguous whether he included armed merchantmen. The German government yielded on May 4 and promised hereafter to observe the rules of visit and search in submarine operations; it added, however, that it reserved liberty of decision if the United States failed to force the British to observe international law. We do not have any clear evidence about Wilson's motives in seemingly risking war during the *Sussex* crisis. Certain inferences from other evidence are, however, clear. Wilson surely hoped as ardently to avoid belligerency in 1916 as he had in 1915, or as he would in early 1917, when confronted with an even more dire German challenge. Why, then, did he run the risk of war over a single incident that could have been passed off as an accident?

The answer is twofold. First, Wilson believed, correctly, that the Germans were about to begin an all-out underseas campaign (under the guise of a campaign against armed merchantmen) that would drive the United States, willy-nilly, into the war. The only way to prevent this catastrophe was to head it off by firm action at a time (as Wilson knew) when the circumstances augured well for the success of a policy of firmness. The Germans had just begun a bloodletting campaign at Verdun; they would soon face (as Wilson also knew) a major British offensive on the Somme. Moreover, as Wilson also undoubtedly knew, the Germans could not mount a truly effective underseas campaign, one successful enough to justify the risk of war with the United States. If Wilson took a calculated risk in laying down the *Sussex* ultimatum, the risk was justified. His *démarche* probably did prevent war between Germany and the United States in 1916.

However, the goal of peace, not merely the prevention of war, was the most compelling objective of Wilson's strong stand in the *Sussex* crisis. House had just returned from London with the House-Grey Memorandum in hand and confident assurances that the British would soon give the signal for its implementation. Wilson fully expected to mount a campaign for mediation in the spring of 1916. A firm stand in the *Sussex* crisis was necessary to assure the British and French that he had the nerve to move decisively for peace.

It should be added that Wilson also carefully gave the Germans an alternative to war. Had Wilson wanted war, he would have followed Lansing's and House's advice, said that any submarine campaign was inherently inhumane and illegal, broken diplomatic relations, and let events take their inevitable course toward war. Wilson did not break relations. He did not denounce the submarine campaign. On the contrary, he made it clear that he would accept submarine operations conducted according to the rules of cruiser warfare.

This concession was more important than most historians have realized. The German leaders carefully avoided any new incident during the summer of 1916; they also greatly augmented their submarine fleet and built new, heavily armed, large U-boats capable of transatlantic operations. Then, in the early autumn of 1916, they launched a highly successful cruiser-type submarine campaign that sent more than one million tons of merchant shipping to the bottom during the last three months of 1916. (Cannon fire accounted for three-quarters of the sinkings.) One submarine, *U-53*, sailed across the Atlantic and took a heavy toll of Allied merchantmen off Newport, Rhode Island. Thus Wilson had not wrested the submarine weapon from German hands. By his policy of severely limiting the armament of merchant ships he had made a successful cruiser-type submarine campaign possible.

With the happy resolution of the *Sussex* crisis, Wilson had completed the task of erecting a solid structure of neutral policies to govern relations between the United States and Great Britain and Germany. Wilson, operating within the limitations imposed by American public opinion, external realities, and, above all, his own conception of the right role of the United States, had made the only kind of adjustments possible in view of the rights and duties of the United States as the leading neutral power. He was now in a position to move on to his next great objective—peace. American neutrality was now, in the spring of 1916, the most hopeful fact of international life.

3

Wilson and the Decisions for War

The interval between about May 1, 1916, and February 1, 1917, was perhaps the most fateful turning point of modern history, because the decisions that the leaders of the great powers made during this period determined the future of mankind for generations to come. It began in despair and gloom: The war had become a bloody stalemate in the trenches, and its continuation could mean only the attrition and perhaps the ruin of western civilization. It ended with at least a semblance of hope: In early 1917 statesmen had an opportunity, under Wilson's leadership, to end the war on terms that might have promised a secure and peaceful future. Wilson made the first decision—to press for mediation under the terms of the House-Grey Memorandum. It was a choice almost foreordained by the events narrated in the preceding chapter. Indeed, Wilson proposed implementation of the memorandum during the height of the *Sussex* crisis. Sir Edward Grey firmly refused, saying that he greatly preferred American entry into the war, and that, in any event, he did not have much hope for Wilson's mediation.

Wilson was undaunted. After all, Colonel House had assured him, and continued to do so, that the British leaders and the usually intransigent French sincerely wanted peace and would cooperate. Wilson returned to the task of getting peace negotiations under way after the *Sussex* crisis. Surely, now, he thought, the time had come to strike for peace. He also began to prepare American public opinion and to give the explicit assurances for postwar security that Sir Edward Grey had earlier demanded. Wilson, in a speech on May 27, 1916, announced the end of American isolation and advocated American membership in a postwar league to maintain the freedom of the seas and the political and territorial integrity of its member nations. He next incorporated a strong league plank in the Democratic platform of 1916.

Meanwhile, from May 10 to July 15, 1916, Wilson applied mounting pressure on the British Foreign Office for implementation of the House-Grey Memorandum. He appealed and pleaded. And he warned that British refusal to cooperate would drive the United States into isolation and compel the Washington government to reexamine its attitudes toward the British maritime system. Wilson explained the situation in a letter to Colonel House on May 16, 1916, as follows:

> We are plainly face to face with this alternative, therefore. The United States must either make a decided move for peace (upon some basis that promises to be permanent) or, if she postpones that, must insist to the limit upon her rights of trade and upon such freedom of the seas as international law already justified her in insisting on as against Great Britain, with the same plain speaking and firmness that she has used against Germany. And the choice must be made immediately. Which does Great Britain prefer? She cannot escape both. To do nothing is now, for us, impossible.

At the outset of these negotiations, Grey tried evasion in order to avoid a rebuffing refusal. He said that the time was not yet ripe for a peace conference, or that the British would have to wait and see the results of the Somme offensive. Grey also urged Wilson to raise the question of peace negotiations with the French government, which Grey knew to be adamantly opposed to any talk of peace. When pressed for a direct answer, Grey finally had to reply frankly that the British and French governments, and not the United States, had the choice under the House-Grey Memorandum of saying when peace talks should begin, and that there was no chance of implementing the memorandum so long as the Allies had any hope of winning a military victory. Worst still for Wilson's hopes, other spokesmen of the British and French governments made it clear that they would regard a mediation move by Wilson as an unfriendly act.

Thus the Allied leaders decided to prolong the war and risk the loss of American friendship and cooperation in the future. This decision was all the more momentous because this was the time, above all others, when Wilson's mediation seemed to have some chance of acceptance by Germany. The civilian leaders in Berlin now had the upper hand in Imperial councils. They saw no way for the Kaiser's armies or his submarines to break the deadlock; they feared that their armies would be unable to withstand the furious Anglo-French pressure on the western front; it might all end in *finis Germaniae.* Consequently, the Imperial Chancellor began to apply heavy pressure on Wilson to make speedy and resolute moves for peace.

The British and French statesmen who refused to join Wilson in a peace *démarche* bear heavy responsibility for the disasters resulting from the prolongation of the war. Sir Edward Grey bears a particular responsibility. From all that we know about his personal attitude (and it comes from Colonel House's diary, which is often unreliable), he favored Anglo-American cooperation for peace. He did present the memorandum to the War Committee of the British cabinet and suggest the wisdom of its implementation. But he did not object when the hardliners vetoed his suggestion. Grey also sent a copy of the memorandum to the French government, but without any hint of endorsement, much less any pressure on the French authorities to consider it seriously. Grey's position all through 1916—and he restated it in a memorandum just before he left office in December 1916—was that American mediation was of course preferable to a German victory, but that the British and French governments should invoke Wilson's intervention only as an alternative to defeat. The misfortune was that Grey, who fully realized the tragedy of the war and the necessity for ending it, had neither the courage nor the resolution to stand down the military leaders and civilian hardliners and insist upon the one instrumentality available for peace.

Perhaps Grey's decision, and the decision of other British leaders (the French never even discussed the House-Grey Memorandum with the British Foreign Office) was inevitable. Perhaps the price of Wilson's mediation was too high and the risks too great. At any rate, by

1916, Allied war objectives were so ambitious that they could have been imposed only upon a beaten foe. In contrast, Wilson's whole policy, as Sir Edward Grey characterized it in his memoirs, "was founded on the assumption that the war was a stalemate, and that the most useful role of the United States was to promote an honourable end without a crushing victory." House had said, during the discussions preceding the initialing of the memorandum, that Wilson would *probably* support the restoration of Belgium, the return of Alsace-Lorraine to France, and Russian control of the Dardanelles. But House never once promised that the United States would fight for even these minimal Allied objectives. House also made it clear that Wilson did not want to see the destruction of German power in Europe, and that the Allies would have to make concessions to Germany as the price for limited gains of their own. House also emphasized that Wilson's great goal—the one for which he was willing to pledge the use of American power to achieve—was a new world security system with guarantees, among others, which would have spelled the doom of British naval supremacy. As Grey also wrote, "If either side, even Germany, were to agree with him in this, he would use the influence of the United States to bring the other side into line. His suggestion of mediation could not be confined to one side."

Second, peace negotiations under Wilson's leadership would have been exceedingly hazardous for the Allies at this time, even if they had been willing to accept a settlement based on the *status quo ante bellum*. In the spring and summer of 1916, the Germans occupied Belgium, northern France, and most of eastern Europe and the Balkans. They would have held most of the trump cards at a peace conference. Therefore, the Allies were understandably reluctant to agree to an armistice without an ironclad promise from Wilson that the United States would enter the war if the Germans refused to evacuate their conquered territories. Wilson never made, and could not constitutionally make, any such commitment. Moreover, his repeated declaration to the effect that he was not concerned about territorial questions, and that the belligerents would have to settle such questions at the peace table among themselves, must have sounded to the Allied leaders as if he did not think that they were worth fighting about.

Third, the British had good reasons to believe that Wilson would not be able, even had he so desired, to bring the United States into the war for the most likely reasons stipulated in the House-Grey Memorandum, namely, German "unreasonableness" in a peace conference. The British Ambassador in Washington, whom Grey trusted implicitly, was reporting at least once a week during the summer of 1916 that Wilson faced certain defeat in the coming presidential election, and so it did appear. Who could guarantee that his successor would not ignore or repudiate the memorandum? There was the even graver danger that Congress would not permit Wilson to fulfill his commitments even if he was reelected. A wave of antiwar sentiment swept through the American people in the summer of 1916. It forced Wilson to conduct his campaign largely on the issue of staying out of the war.

Finally, although French cooperation was vital to the implementation of the House-Grey Memorandum, House had made it certain that the French would ignore that document. House made the inconceivable mistake of considering France a second-class power, subject to dictates from London. He thought that all he had to do in Paris was to implant confidence in Wilson among the leaders of the French government, so that they would follow the English lead when Grey said the word for peace. Hence House did not even broach with the French the plan that would be embodied in the memorandum. Instead, he said that the United States wanted to do everything possible to help the Allies win the war; (contrary to Wilson's explicit instructions) that the Allies should tighten their blockade; and that the United States would be in the war militarily on the Allied side by the autumn of 1916, regardless of the state of Allied military fortunes. (Needless to say, House never reported these statements to Wilson.) The French were astonished but not deceived by House's assurances. They did not want Wilson's mediation; they did not expect military assistance from the United States; and they were determined to fight the war to a finish or perish in the process.

Wilson's response to Grey's refusal to implement the House-

51

Grey Memorandum was to set under way plans to build a navy to rival the British fleet, to strengthen American neutrality through legislation that could be used to bring the Allies to book, and, finally, to press forward in his own independent campaign for peace. It was the grand culmination of all of his strategy and plans since 1914. It was also the almost inevitable outgrowth of events at home and abroad that converged to produce a radical change in American foreign policy.

One of these events was Wilson's mounting anger (the word is used advisedly) with the British on account of their rejection, as he thought, of his right hand of fellowship. This anger helped to produce in Wilson a growing suspicion of the merits of the Allied cause and beliefs powerful enough to affect his foreign policy—that the Allies were fighting for conquest and domination and preferred to prolong the carnage rather than to consent to a fair and liberal peace sentiment.

A serious deterioration in the official relations of the United States and Great Britain from the spring of 1916 onward also encouraged the bitterness in Washington and speeded the change of policy. To state the matter simply, Grey had lost control, and the Admiralty and Ministry of Blockade tightened the British maritime system to the point of denying the last vestiges of neutral rights. They also engaged in practices that seemed to strike at American fundamental rights, independence, and national dignity. They touched the sensitive nerve of American pride.

Among other things, the British began to search, seize, and censor American transatlantic mail. They carried their economic warfare to the territory of the United States by issuing a "blacklist" of American firms suspected of trading with the Central Powers and forbade British subjects to deal with these firms. They sought to bring all American shipping under the British Admiralty's control by denying American shipmasters the right to buy coal in British ports around the world if they refused to sail under the Admiralty's instructions.

Another cause of the growing anti-British revulsion in Washington and the United States was the ruthless British suppression of the Irish rebellion on Easter Day, April 24, 1916. Irish independence fighters proclaimed the Irish Republic and occupied certain government buildings. The British army drove them out in bloody fighting, rounded up the ringleaders, and summarily shot them. "The Dublin executions," exclaimed *The New Republic,* the leading American journal of opinion, "have done more to drive America back to isolation than any other event since the war began." Sentiment was further exacerbated when the British hanged one of the leading Irish rebels, Sir Roger Casement, in spite of an appeal for clemency from the United States Senate. Irish-Americans were in a frenzy of fury, while a wave of anger swept through all major segments of American opinion.

These events contributed to an extraordinary outburst of neutralism among Americans during the summer of 1916. But the main reason for this surge of antiwar sentiment was the daily news of the increasing carnage on the western front, the belief that the war was endless, and the still prevailing conviction that American security would not be threatened whatever the outcome in Europe. Neutralism became the reigning passion in the United States during the summer and autumn of 1916. It silenced the few outright interventionists who existed; destroyed politically the one leader, Theodore Roosevelt, who defied its power; and engulfed both political parties. Most important, it convinced Wilson that the vast majority of Americans would not want to go to war if the Germans violated the *Sussex* pledge and sank *belligerent* merchantmen without warning.

The decisive forces that drove Wilson toward an independent campaign for peace were his knowledge that the war was entering a new and more desperate phase and his fear that it might be impossible for the United States to avoid the cross fire. Congress and the American people might drive him into war in sheer anger. Then they would be fighting blindly in defense of national rights, without any long-range objectives—and only with the result that one side would win a smashing victory and be able to impose a Carthaginian settlement that would make a new war inevitable within another generation.

Wilson expressed these fears poignantly in the draft of a peace note that he composed (but did not send) soon after his reelection in November 1916:

53

> The position of the neutral nations . . . has been rendered all but intolerable. Their commerce is interrupted, their industries are checked and diverted, the lives of their people are put in constant jeopardy, they are virtually forbidden the accustomed highways of the sea. . . . If any other nation now neutral should be drawn in, it would know only that it was drawn in by some force it could not resist, because it had been hurt and saw no remedy but to risk still greater, it might be even irreparable injury, in order to make the weight in the one scale or the other decisive; and even as a participant it would not know how far the scales must tip before the end would come or what was being weighed in the balance!

It was to avoid this predicament that Wilson set out upon his new course.

His first move was to take the steps necessary to bring the Allies under his complete control. There were verbal warnings to London from the State Department. They were no longer written in friendly language. On the contrary, they accused the British government of "lawless" conduct and warned that the United States would not tolerate the continuation of "repeated violations of international law." At the same time, Wilson, in September, asked for and obtained legislation from Congress to give him drastic retaliatory powers. This legislation empowered him to deny port facilities and clearance to the ships of any nation that discriminated against firms in the United States or violated the rights of American shippers at sea; to levy an embargo against any nation that denied American trading rights under international law; and to deny the use of American mail and communications systems to any nation that interfered with American mail or communications. Moreover, the legislation authorized Wilson to use the armed forces of the United States to enforce these provisions.

Wilson's most drastic measure was action severely to curtail, if not end, private American loans to the Allies. The Anglo-French loan of 1915 had been a complete disaster. Of the $500 million in bonds issued, only $33 million had been bought by private investors. Six companies with large contracts with the British government had helped by buying about $100 million of the bonds; but the underwriters had to take up the balance of $187 million of unsold bonds. The failure of the loan proved that the American people would not support the Allied war effort from their own resources, nor would American banks lend on unsecured treasury notes and bonds. To be sure, the flow of credit did not stop. Between the autumn of 1915 and the winter of 1916, the British (also the chief creditor of all the Allies) borrowed about $2 billion in the United States. However, the British Treasury gave high-grade American, Canadian, and Latin-American collateral against all these loans. These resources were near depletion by the autumn of 1916. The British government's financial agent in the United States, J. P. Morgan and Company, then resorted to the expedient of accepting large quantities of renewable short-term British Treasury notes. These in turn were sold to American banks to finance Allied purchases.

The members of the Federal Reserve Board were profoundly concerned, not merely about the liquidity of the British short-term notes, but also about the growing dependence of the American economy upon the war trade. The chairman of the board drafted a statement cautioning American banks and took it to the White House on November 25. Wilson said that he liked the statement but thought that it should be stronger. The chairman issued a revised statement, which Wilson had read and approved, on November 27. The statement, sent to member banks of the Federal Reserve System, said that the Federal Reserve Board did not "regard it in the interest of the country at this time that they invest in foreign Treasury bills of this character."

Wilson now had the power of life or death over the Allies. An investigation by the various departments of the British government following the adoption of the American retaliatory legislation had revealed this dependence in complete detail. British gold and other reserves would be utterly exhausted by April 1, 1917; after that date, a Treasury official said, Great Britain and the Allies would be at the mercy of the President of the United States. Wilson probably did not know the precise details. But he did know that he had the power absolutely to coerce the Allies.

Wilson possessed no such power over Germany, but that did not seem to matter since Bethmann Hollweg had been increasing his pressure on Wilson to move speedily for peace. Indeed, the Chancellor sent the American Ambassador to Germany on a special mission to Washington to urge Wilson to act.

The opportunity for which Wilson had been working since the outbreak of the war seemed to be at hand, and he began preparations for his independent mediation immediately after his reelection. Protracted discussions among Wilson, Lansing, and House disclosed the opportunities and dangers of independent mediation. The Allies were now even more violently opposed than before to peace talks. The German leaders, in contrast, were not only begging Wilson to call a peace conference, but were even ready, so Bernstorff said, to evacuate Belgium and France in return for an armistice. What would happen, Lansing and House asked, if Germany responded favorably to a call for peace and the Allies rejected it? Might not the United States drift into a sympathetic alliance with Germany and into a naval war with England and Japan? Would it not be safer, House asked, to revive the House-Grey Memorandum and to move for mediation under its terms?

Wilson, somewhat curtly, turned aside all such suggestions. Old plans like the House-Grey Memorandum, based upon secret Anglo-American cooperation, he exclaimed, were out of date. He would not, in any event, be burned again. He had to stand for peace alone. He had to be a truly independent mediator. He would work with the Germans if they were willing to cooperate with him. If the Allies would not cooperate, he would coerce them into cooperation.

Wilson did not think that the risk of rupture and war with the Allies was very great. He did not believe that they were intent on suicide. "This morning in discussing these matters with the President," House wrote in his diary on November 15, 1916, "he went so far as to say that if the Allies wanted war with us we would not shrink from it. . . . He thought they would not dare resort to this and if they did, they could do this country no serious hurt."

The German military leaders believed that they faced ultimate defeat if they could not obtain peace in the near future. If the Allies were adamant, then the Germans had one last desperate chance—an all-out submarine campaign to end the war quickly. They also believed that Wilson would not take the initiative for peace. Consequently, the German High Command agreed to permit the Chancellor to move on his own; but they warned him that failure of the Allies to respond positively would necessitate resort to their *ultima ratio.*

The Chancellor issued his call on December 12, and it galvanized Wilson into action. He sent a message to the belligerent capitals on December 18. In order to avoid giving the appearance of supporting the German call, Wilson eliminated the demand in his original draft for assembling a peace conference. However, he wrote movingly of the plight of the neutrals, of the tragedy and terrors of a war that threatened the ruin of Europe, and of the dire need for a return of peace. All of the belligerents, according to their official statements and pronouncements, he said, were fighting for the same objectives. He ended by asking the belligerents to state frankly the terms upon which they would agree to end the war.

Lansing, deeply emotionally committed to American intervention in order to guarantee an Allied victory, now intervened in one of the most egregious acts of treachery in American history in an effort to torpedo Wilson's peace move. On the same day that Wilson's peace note appeared in the newspapers, December 21, Lansing issued a statement saying that the United States was "drawing nearer the verge of war" and had to know what the rival alliances were fighting for in order to determine its own policies. A furious Wilson forced Lansing to publish a halfway retraction in the newspapers on the following day. However, on December 20 and 22, Lansing had talked to the French and British Ambassadors. He was of course speaking only privately, Lansing said; nonetheless, he thought that the Allies, in their reply to Wilson, might rightfully demand the return of Alsace-Lorraine to France, a considerable indemnity for France, Belgium, and Serbia, and the settlement of Balkan questions by an international commission. Above all, the Allies should make it clear that they would negotiate only with a reformed and democratized Germany. (These, of course, were terms that could be achieved only by a smashing Allied victory.)

The motives for Lansing's betrayal can be reasonably inferred. As has been said, he was committed heart and soul to the Allied cause; he also believed that Allied victory was essential to the security of the United States. He knew, on a basis of good intelligence reports from

Berlin, that the desperate German military leaders would resort to an all-out submarine campaign if the Allies failed to return a conciliatory reply to Germany's call for peace conference and Wilson's appeal for a statement of terms. He also thought that an all-out submarine campaign would probably drive the United States into the war on the Allied side. Hence we can only conclude that Lansing was maneuvering to force the Germans into war with the United States.

The German government responded first to Wilson on December 26. After thanking Wilson for his noble initiative, it added that peace terms would best be worked out through a direct exchange between the belligerents. Two days later, the leaders of the British and French governments met in London on December 28 to frame a joint Anglo-French reply and to discuss matters of military strategy. Both the French and British minutes of this meeting reveal that the conferees devoted very little time to the reply to Wilson. The British and French leaders discussed Lansing's messages and decided without much ado to follow his advice. The terms listed in the Anglo-French reply, sent to Wilson on January 10, 1917, were virtually the same ones that Lansing had suggested. At the same time, they drafted a reply to the German government's call for a peace conference. Sent to Berlin by way of Washington on December 29, it said that the Allies would not consider any German offer as genuine unless it was accompanied by a statement of terms.

Actually, it was the Anglo-French response to the German peace offer that brought matters to a head in Germany. All top German civilian and military leaders met with the Kaiser at his eastern headquarters in Pless Castle in Silesia on January 9. Naval spokesmen, armed with elaborate memoranda, guaranteed absolutely that an unrestricted submarine campaign against all maritime commerce, belligerent *and* neutral, could reduce Great Britain to starvation and surrender within five months. It was impossible to exempt neutral ships because they constituted one-third of the tonnage sailing to the British Isles; the submarine campaign would fail if they were free to bring in life-sustaining supplies. Bethmann Hollweg still believed that an all-out campaign would bring the United States into the war and that American intervention would mean the end of Germany. But he was exhausted after so many months of struggle against the military leaders and knew that he had lost the Kaiser's confidence. Resistance was useless, indeed would only mean his ouster. The Secretary of the Treasury, Karl Helfferich, pointed out that the Admiralty had taken no account of the possibility of the development of effective anti-submarine measures; moreover, he warned, the American Civil War had proved that Americans, once aroused, would never stop fighting until they had won. No one listened to him. The Kaiser decreed that the all-out campaign should begin on February 1, 1917. Meanwhile, unrestricted warfare against armed merchantmen should begin at once.

In retrospect, it would appear that this, the most fateful decision made by any government during the war, was inevitable. At least the men who made the decision thought that they had no alternative. Their foes seemed to be implacable. Moreover, the Admiralty's arguments seemed convincing. It now had the capacity to establish an effective blockade of the British Isles, for it could keep about twenty-five submarines in western waters and the Mediterranean at the same time by February 1, and a growing number after that date. Moreover, a short wheat crop in the Americas augured well for the success of the blockade. Germany, it seemed, had a chance to win a total victory and a settlement that would establish German supremacy in Europe. The decision made at Pless Castle was the only one that offered any hope to the army commanders. They had long since lost hope of winning the war in the trenches; indeed, they were convinced that Germany would lose the war without resort to the submarine weapon. No military (or civilian) leaders involved in a war for survival have ever refused to use any weapon that promised quick and overwhelming victory.

Fear of an American declaration of war, heretofore the chief constraint upon the submarine campaign, no longer had any effect on German policy. All German leaders assumed that a wholesale attack on American ships would drive the United States into the war. But, it seemed certain, American belligerency would not make any difference. Indeed, it would have certain positive advantages. It would cause the diversion of huge quantities of food and war material to an American army in training during the very period when the U-boats would be winning the war on the seas.

59

As we now know, the German decision at Pless was also one of the greatest blunders in history. As we will see, Wilson would almost certainly have accepted an all-out submarine campaign against *belligerent* merchantmen, exclusive, perhaps, of unarmed passenger ships, and such a campaign could have been devastating, perhaps decisive. American public opinion was overwhelmingly opposed to war; Congress certainly would not have adopted a war resolution over the issue of the safety of belligerent merchantmen and the right of a few Americans to work on them. But Wilson would not have asked for a declaration of war over this issue. His determination to avoid belligerency had never been stronger than at this very time. "There will be no war," he told Colonel House on January 4, 1917. "This country does not intend to become involved in this war. . . . It would be a crime against civilization for us to go in." Moreover, if the German leaders had postponed their decision for six months (or less), it would have been unnecessary. War exports from the United States to the Allies would have been reduced to a trickle by April on account of the breakdown of the Anglo-American system of exchange. Russian resistance would have collapsed by late summer and enabled the Germans to concentrate their armies on the western front.

Thus we were faced with one of the supreme ironies of history. By doing the thing that seemed to guarantee victory, the Germans made their own defeat inevitable. By failing to adopt limited policies, they threw away their chance of success. On the other hand, as Bethmann Hollweg wrote in his memoirs, hindsight is a great deal easier than foresight.

But we are getting ahead somewhat of our story, because Wilson gave the Germans an opportunity to reverse the decision made at Pless and to choose peace instead of war with the United States. Undismayed by the German refusal to divulge peace terms, Wilson pushed forward by beginning high-level secret negotiations with the British and German governments.

Colonel House put the pressure on Bernstorff first—on December 27, 1916. The Ambassador cabled at once to Berlin. He said that Wilson was eager to begin negotiations but had to know the German terms. Bernstorff added that Wilson was not much interested in territorial questions but was much concerned about guarantees for future peace. Bethmann drafted a positive response; then, losing his nerve, he permitted the dispatch of a reply prepared by the new German Foreign Secretary, Arthur Zimmermann. It said, clearly, so that it could not be misunderstood, that Germany did not desire Wilson's participation in the conference that would end the war. It added that German terms were moderate as compared with the Entente's and did not include the annexation of Belgium. Moreover, Bernstorff should assure Wilson that Germany would gladly furnish all the postwar guarantees that he desired.

Bernstorff relayed only the positive part of this message to House on January 15. Wilson was excited and all the more eager to obtain early agreement with Berlin because he feared that the Anglo-French terms, just published, would push the scales in Germany completely in favor of the military party. Wilson was startled if not shocked by the pretentiousness of the Allied demands. They were impossible and mainly bluff, he thought. He feared that the Allied note might slam the door to peace if he did not move quickly.

Discouraging news came in a letter from Bernstorff to House on January 19. It repeated the Ambassador's early assurances of German willingness to welcome Wilson's leadership in a conference to reconstruct the international order. However, it added what Bernstorff had failed to tell House earlier—that a conference limited to the belligerents would have to meet first and conclude a peace settlement *before* the postwar conference could assemble.

Wilson had meanwhile been hard at work on the second part of his grand strategy for peace—a statement to the world of the kind of peace settlement that the United States could approve and would join a league of nations to support. It was also to be a message to the *peoples* of the warring countries. But speed was of the essence. Hence, Wilson finished the document on about January 12, made arrangements to deliver it in the form of an address to the Senate, sent it to the belligerent capitals on January 15, and instructed American ambassadors to arrange for its publication in the newspapers.

Wilson read his address to the Senate in the early afternoon of January 22. The great question, he said, was whether the war was a struggle for a just and secure peace, or only for a new balance of power. The peace to be made had to be "a peace without victory," a "peace among equals," one that would confer a common benefit upon all mankind. He continued:

> Victory would mean peace forced upon the loser, a victor's terms imposed upon the vanquished. It would be accepted in humiliation, under duress, at an intolerable sacrifice, and would leave a sting, a resentment, a bitter memory upon which terms of peace would rest, not permanently, but only as upon quicksand.

Wilson then went on to describe the kind of settlement that the American people and, as he put it, "the silent mass of mankind in every nation" yearned for and would support in the future.*

The British replied first, on January 26, through Sir William Wiseman, head of British naval intelligence in the United States. House had been negotiating with him to obtain British consent to an early peace conference. (The British Ambassador, Sir Cecil Spring Rice, had long since lost Wilson's and House's confidence on account of his volatility and outbursts against American policies.) Wiseman told House that he was in direct and confidential communication with the Foreign Office. He thought that an early peace conference could be arranged provided the Germans responded favorably to Wilson's overtures. "He went so far," House reported to Wilson, "as to discuss with me where the conference should be held. . . . I take it he has heard directly from his government since yesterday for he seemed to speak with authority." The records relating to the British response have been destroyed, and it is possible that Wiseman was speaking on his own. However, Wiseman was the personal liaision between the new British Prime Minister and Foreign Secretary, David Lloyd George and Arthur Balfour, respectively; it is inconceivable that Wiseman should have spoken without authority.

The reasons for British willingness to go to the peace table under Wilson's aegis are mutually supportive. British intelligence was superb, and officials in London knew that the Germans had decided to launch an all-out submarine campaign. However, they could not have

*See p. 75.

been certain that this would drive Wilson into the war. As has been said, the British financial situation was desperate at this time. Moreover, the danger of Russian collapse and withdrawal from the war was ominously real. Finally, the British knew that Germany now had the capacity to conduct a devastating submarine campaign. Thus, it is altogether possible that British leaders had come to Sir Edward Grey's conclusion that Wilsonian mediation was preferable to defeat.

Actually, it mattered little at this point what the British said to Wilson, or why they said it. Wilson had the power of life or death over the Allies and was prepared to use it to force them to the peace table. Everything now depended upon the Germans. As Wilson put it in a letter to Colonel House on January 24:

> If Germany really wants peace she can get it, and get it soon, *if she will but confide in me and let me have a chance....* It occurs to me that it would be well for you to see Bernstorff again, at once.... and tell him that this is the time to accomplish something, if they really and truly want peace; that the indications that have come to us are of a sort to lead us to believe that with something reasonable to suggest, as from them, I can bring things about.... Feelings, exasperations are neither here nor there. Do they in fact want me to help? I am entitled to know because I genuinely want to help and have now put myself in a position to help without favour to either side.

House relayed Wilson's message urgently to Bernstorff on January 26, and the Ambassador sent it to Berlin over the State Department's wire on the following day. Wilson offered his mediation upon a basis of his address to the Senate, Bernstorff's message said. The Allied terms were impossible; in any event they were "a bluff" and need not be taken into consideration. Wilson was certain that he could bring about both peace conferences. But Germany had to disclose its terms and trust him. Bernstorff added his own plea for acceptance of Wilson's offer and for postponement of the submarine campaign, about which he had earlier been informed.

This was the most important communication between Washington and Berlin since the beginning of the war. It offered Wilson's right hand of cooperation in what could have been an irresistible move for peace, a "peace without victory," and a new chance for mankind. The choice between war and peace was now up to the Germans.

Bethmann received Bernstorff's telegram on January 29. In a state of great excitement, the Chancellor took a special train to Pless, summoned an Imperial conference, and laid out his plan. It was to divulge German terms and urge Wilson to continue his efforts for peace. Meanwhile, the submarine campaign would go forward on schedule; perhaps it would be so effective that the United States would not want to enter the war. The Kaiser agreed; however, he insisted that the Chancellor make it plain that he would not accept Wilson as a mediator.

Bernstorff handed three communications to Lansing on January 31. The first was an announcement that submarines would, on February 1, begin an unrestricted campaign against all shipping, belligerent and neutral, in a broad zone around the British Isles, France, and Italy, and in the eastern Mediterranean. There would be a period of grace for neutral ships at sea. Moreover, one American passenger ship might sail each way between New York and England, provided that the ships were clearly marked and did not carry contraband. The second was a letter from Bernstorff to Lansing intended for publication. It affirmed Germany's adherence to the ideals enunciated in Wilson's address to the Senate, said that the Allies had made clear their intention to dismember and dishonor the Central Powers, and appealed for a continuation of American neutrality in order to avoid further bloodshed.

The third communication was a personal confidential message from Bethmann to Wilson. Germany, it said, welcomed and would support Wilson's efforts to force the Allies to "a direct conference of the belligerents." However, the Allied terms were no bluff, and the Allies would regard disclosure of German terms as a sign of weakness. Then, for Wilson's "own personal information," the Chancellor listed the terms upon which Germany would have been willing to negotiate if the Allies had responded to Germany's peace appeal of December 12. They were harsh enough to have been rejected out of hand by the Allies. Bethmann did not tell Wilson that Germany and Austria-Hungary had recently agreed on additional terms that would have made Belgium a vassal state and partially dismembered Russia. The Chancellor concluded by saying that it might have been possible to postpone the new U-boat campaign if Wilson's message had come a few days earlier; however, the submarines were already at sea with their instructions. Germany wanted to do full justice to the United States as far as possible. It hoped that the President would continue his efforts; and it stood ready to discontinue the submarine campaign if Wilson could give assurances that he could obtain a peace settlement *satisfactory to Germany.*

Wilson was stunned and so much in despair that, for once, he did not know what to do. He said to House that it seemed as if the world had started turning in an opposite direction. Lansing and House advised an immediate break in relations, but Wilson hesitated to take any step that might lead to war. As he told Lansing, he would go to almost any lengths "rather than to have this nation actually involved in the conflict." At a cabinet meeting on February 2, Wilson said that he had been astounded by the German announcement; that he would like to see the neutrals unite; and that he did not wish either side to win because greater justice would be done if the war ended in a draw.

After the cabinet meeting, in the late afternoon, Wilson went to the President's Room in the Capitol and summoned the members of the Senate Foreign Relations Committee to come and advise him what to do. Sixteen Democratic senators came (no Republicans could be found). Two of them advised waiting until Germany committed an overt act; all the rest said that it was obvious what the Germans were going to do, and that Wilson should break relations at once.

Hence Wilson went before a joint session of Congress on the following day and announced that he had instructed the Secretary of State to give the German Ambassador his passports and inform him that all diplomatic relations between the United States and Germany were severed. However, the balance of the address revealed that he had found an alternative to war, at least if the Germans would accept it. His words made it clear that he would accept the new German submarine campaign provided that the Germans did not sink *American* ships without warning. He said that he refused to believe that the German authorities would pay no regard to the ancient friendship between the German and American peoples or to the solemn promises that they had made to the American government and ruthlessly destroy American ships and American lives on the high seas. Only "actual overt acts" could make him believe that "even now." He explained what he would do should his confidence in the sobriety and prudence of the German leaders be unfounded:

> I shall take the liberty of coming again before the Congress, to ask that authority be given me to use any means that may be necessary for the protection of our seamen and our people in the prosecution of their peaceful and legitimate errands on the high seas.

In short, Wilson was saying that he would follow a policy of watchful waiting and govern his future policies in response to what the Germans did. He would not go to war because the Germans had violated the *Sussex* pledge. He would do nothing if they spared American ships of all categories and, presumably, American lives on belligerent passenger ships. If the Germans attacked American ships, he would protect them by an armed neutrality. This, obviously, was not the language of war, but of peace if peace was at all possible.

Throughout the first weeks of February 1917, Wilson waited patiently to see what the future would bring. At any moment the German government could have removed the possibility of war by announcing that it would respect American shipping and take all possible precautions to protect American lives on passenger ships.

Two events greatly excited Wilson's hopes during the first two weeks of February. One was the receipt of an extraordinary message from Count Ottokar Czernin, the Austro-Hungarian Foreign Minister. It said that Austria-Hungary was prepared to accept a peace without victory and begged Wilson to try to induce the Allies to accept the same point of view. Wilson at once sent a telegram to London urging the British to give assurances that they would not insist upon the dismemberment of the Hapsburg empire. The second event was Bernstorff's (he did not leave Washington until February 14) effort to reopen negotiations between Washington and Berlin through the Swiss Minister. All that was required to preserve peace with the United States, Bernstorff said, was safety for American shipping. But all reason had fled the minds of the German leaders. They severely scolded Czernin. And they rebuffed Bernstorff's suggestion with the reply that not even the reestablishment of diplomatic relations with the United States would cause the German government to reconsider "its resolution to completely stop by submarines all importations from abroad by its enemies."

Despite the obvious German determination to enforce a total blockade, Wilson refused to permit the defense departments to make any important preparations for war. Goods now piled up on American docks as American shipmasters refused to leave the safety of their harbors. As the days passed, the pressures for the adoption of at least an armed neutrality mounted irresistibly. Moreover, leading antiwar spokesmen were proposing armed neutrality as the best and most sensible alternative to full-scale belligerency.

Here, indeed, was the alternative that Wilson had been looking for. Thus he went to Congress on February 26 and requested authority to put naval gun crews on American merchantmen and to "employ any other instrumentalities or methods that may be necessary and adequate to protect our ships and our people in their legitimate and peaceful pursuits on the seas." He carefully explained that he was not contemplating war or any steps that might lead to war. "I merely request," he said,

> that you will accord me by your own vote and definite bestowal the means and the authority to safeguard in practice the right of a great people who are at peace and who are desirous of exercising none but the rights of peace to follow the pursuits of peace in quietness and good will—rights recognized time out of mind by all the civilized nations of the world. No course of my choosing or of theirs will lead to war. War can come only by the willful acts and aggressions of others.

(Wilson was extraordinarily self-revealing in his language. The reader will have noted the use of the word "peace" three times in the first sentence quoted above.)

A small group of senators, by a filibuster at the end of the session, prevented passage of a measure authorizing Wilson to arm merchantmen. He took this action anyway on March 9, 1917, under authority of an old antipiracy statute. At the same time, he called Congress into special session for April 16, presumably to sanction a more elaborate program of armed neutrality, on which he set to work at once with the Navy Department.

By mid-March, therefore, it seemed that Wilson had made a firm decision in favor of a defensive war on the seas. "We stand firm in armed neutrality," he declared, for example, in his second inaugural address on March 5, "since it seems that in no other way we can demonstrate what it is we insist upon and cannot forego." Yet on April 2 (he had meanwhile convened Congress for this earlier date), less than a month after he uttered these words, he stood before Congress and asked for a declaration of war. What events occurred, what forces were at work, what pressures were applied during these few weeks to cause Wilson to make the decision that he had been trying desperately to avoid? No statesman has ever gone through as much agony and self-doubt in deciding for war. Wilson was reluctant up to the very end. So we should put the question another way: What caused Wilson to abandon armed neutrality and decide that he had no alternative but to *accept* the decision for war?

There was first the fact that, from the end of February through the first three weeks in March, the Germans pressed a relentless, total underseas attack against all ships passing through the war zones. They sank the British liner *Laconia* without warning on February 25 with the loss of two American lives. Between March 16 and March 18, submarines sank three American merchantmen—*City of Memphis, Illinois,* and *Vigilancia*—the latter two without warning and the third with heavy loss of life. These incidents, to say nothing of slashing attacks against other neutral and belligerent ships, removed all doubt from Wilson's mind that the Germans were deadly serious in their intent to destroy all commerce and human life in the broad war zones.

The clearer the character of the unlimited submarine campaign became, the stronger Wilson's conviction grew that armed neutrality would not suffice to protect American commerce. Nor did it seem a legally possible instrumentality. Placement of naval gun crews on ships carrying contraband to the Allies was, technically, an act of war.

Moreover, the German Admiralty announced that the captured crews of armed American ships would be treated as pirates.

Wilson explained these difficulties in his war message, as follows:

> When I addressed the Congress on the 26th of February last, I thought that it would suffice to assert our neutral rights with arms. . . . But armed neutrality, it now appears, is impracticable. Because submarines are in effect outlaws when used as the German submarines have been used against merchant shipping, it is impossible to defend ships against their attacks as the law of nations has assumed that merchantmen would defend themselves. . . . It is common prudence in such circumstances, grim necessity indeed, to endeavor to destroy them before they show their own intention. . . . The German Government denies the right of neutrals to use arms at all within the areas of the sea which it has proscribed. . . . The intimation is conveyed that the armed guards which we have placed on our own merchant ships will be treated as beyond the pale of law and subject to be dealt with as pirates would be. Armed neutrality is ineffectual enough at best; in such circumstances and in the face of such pretensions it is worse than ineffectual; it is likely only to produce what it was meant to prevent; it is practically certain to draw us into the war without either the rights or the effectiveness of belligerents.

This passage reveals the *immediate* reason why Wilson accepted the decision for war. It was simply that the German assault upon American lives and property was so overwhelming and so flagrant a denial of national rights that armed neutrality was both ineffective and inappropriate. "I would be inclined to adopt . . . [armed neutrality]," Wilson had written only two days before he delivered his war message, "indeed, as you know, I had already adopted it, but this is the difficulty: . . . To make even the measures of defense legitimate we must obtain the status of belligerents."

In light of what we know about Wilson's convictions and high goals, however, it seems safe to assume that, had not other events, pressures, and ambitions persuaded him to accept the decision for war, he would have persevered in armed neutrality and avoided full-scale belligerency. Indeed, before the break in diplomatic relations he had told Lansing that if "it was for the good of the world for the United States to keep out of the war in the present circumstances, he would be willing to bear all the criticism and abuse which would surely follow our failure to break with Germany."

The combined weight of official and public opinion was one pressure driving Wilson toward acceptance of belligerency. It was a fact of great consequence that, at the cabinet meeting of March 20, when the issue of war or peace was fully debated, every cabinet member, including those who had heretofore opposed bellicose measures, advised Wilson to admit that a state of war with Germany already existed. Public opinion had remained stubbornly pacific until the end of February. Then the publication of the Zimmermann telegram (in which Germany proposed to Mexico an alliance against the United States and promised the return of Texas, New Mexico, and Arizona) and, above all, the destruction of American ships after mid-March generated a mounting demand for war in all sections and among all classes, until it *seemed* to be a national and majority demand. Enthusiasm for war was further stimulated by news of the overthrow of the czarist regime and the establishment of a provisional democratic government in Russia. This news may have convinced many wavering Americans, but certainly not Wilson, that the Allies were indeed fighting for democracy. However, the war movement at home did not push a hesitant President over the brink. He had more than enough moral strength and courage to withstand any popular demand, even if it had been the demand of the majority. But the country was still deeply divided over the issue of belligerency; all the evidence that we have indicates that a majority of Americans were opposed to fighting. Wilson knew this better than anyone else.

More important was the fact that, by late March 1917, Wilson had lost all faith in the integrity, credibility, and good intentions of the German leaders. As he said, correctly, in his war message, Germany was ruled by a military autocracy which was not responsible to the German people. Many times it had violated American neutrality on American soil. It had tried to lure Mexico into war against its neighbor. It had broken all its solemn pledges to the United States. Worst of all, it was striking out for world dominion. All these convictions, while important, were probably not determinative with Wilson. He had little more confidence in the Allied governments, particularly the British, than in the German government. Wilson accepted belligerency primarily for two other reasons. One was his conviction, widely shared by his contemporaries, that the war was in its final stages and that the people of Europe could not endure the bloodletting and terror much longer. The Germans would shoot their submarine bolt and fail; the Allies would try one last unsuccessful offensive on the western front. In these circumstances, decisive American participation would greatly hasten the end of the ghastly carnage.

But the compelling reason for Wilson's decision to accept belligerency was his conviction that only by going to war could he win the goals for which he had been working since August 1914—a reasonable peace settlement and the reconstruction of the world order. As he told a group of antiwar leaders on February 28, "as head of a nation participating in the war, the President of the United States would have a seat at the Peace Table, but . . . [as] the representative of a neutral country he could at best only 'call through a crack in the door.' "

To wage war in order to make peace—that was Wilson's intention. God had created the United States in order to serve civilization and mankind. Now the test had come, and America was privileged to "spend her blood and her might for the principles that gave her birth and happiness and the peace which she has treasured." God helping her, she could do no other.

4

Wilson and the Liberal Peace Program

Never before had the tasks of leadership in foreign affairs been so difficult for Woodrow Wilson than they became after the adoption by Congress of the war resolution on April 6, 1917. His task was to articulate the war aims of the United States and to give voice to the aspirations of peoples everywhere for a hopeful future, without driving a fatal wedge between his country and the Allies in a war against a common foe. His was also the even more arduous and difficult task, once the war had ended, of achieving a "peace without victory," in spite of the primal passions set loose by years of bloodshed and by ambitions multiplied by victory.

The challenges were great, but so, also, were Wilson's courage and faith during the campaign that he waged for the ideals that he conceived to be the cornerstone of a just and lasting peace. Let us now see how Wilson tried to free mankind from the grip of past predatory practices and behavior in international relations.

Wilson had a highly creative mind and was undoubtedly the chief innovator of what we will call, for purposes of brevity, the liberal peace program. But he made his chief contribution to the development of that program by synthesizing widely held hopes, plans, and programs; by expressing them in words that moved the hearts of people all over the world; and by devising the practical means to achieve them.

No sooner had the war begun in the summer of 1914 than men

and women in Europe and the United States began to talk about peace and ways to prevent future wars. These international liberals drew upon common Judeo-Christian values and humanitarian traditions and, regardless of their nationality, proposed virtually the same plans for a peace settlement and reconstruction of the world over. First, all liberals demanded an end to entangling alliances, secret diplomacy, and attempts to maintain balances of power. Liberals were convinced that this—the old diplomacy—had made war inevitable in 1914. Instead they wanted open diplomacy, democratically controlled, and a concert of power instead of rival balances of power. For example, the platform of the Union of Democratic control, the leading British pacifist organization, read:

> The foreign policy of Great Britain shall not be aimed at creating alliances for the purpose of maintaining the "balance of power," but shall be directed to the establishment of a concert of the powers and the setting up of an international council whose deliberations and decisions shall be public.

Second, all international liberals were convinced that the existence of large armies and navies was a prime cause of war. Consequently, they demanded such sweeping reductions in armaments as would leave each nation with only that military power necessary to maintain domestic order. Some peace organizations, like the Women's Peace Party of the United States, also demanded the nationalization of the manufacture of armaments; others, like the International Peace Bureau of Belgium, wanted strict international control. In addition, most liberals favored the internationalization of great waterways like the Panama, Suez, and Kiel canals and of strategic points like Gibraltar and the Bosporus.

Third, most liberals envisaged the creation of a postwar international organization strong enough to preserve peace and prevent aggression. The South German Social Democrats proposed a confederacy of all European states and a worldwide alliance against aggression. The League to Enforce Peace, organized in the United States in 1915, proposed a league whose members would be bound to use their economic and military resources against an aggressor. The League of Nations Association, founded in Great Britain in 1915, also worked for the creation of such an organization.

As a first step toward achieving these grand objectives, most international liberals demanded an end to the war and a settlement based on the principles of no indemnities, self-determination or autonomy for subject peoples, no transfer of territory without the consent of the peoples involved, and plebiscites to determine the fate of Alsace-Lorraine and Ireland.

Liberals in the belligerent countries worked against fearful odds, but Wilson kept in close communication with them, particularly the British, through Colonel House from 1914 to 1917. The wheels of history (or perhaps we should say of peace) began to move significantly when Wilson began to take leadership in the movement for a liberal peace program. This happened in the following way.

Before House went to Europe in 1916, Sir Edward Grey said that the British government might be willing to accept Wilson's mediation, provided that the United States would agree to join a postwar league committed to disarmament and to the territorial integrity of member nations. "How much are the United States prepared to do in this direction?" Grey asked House in a letter in September 1915. "Would the President propose that there should be a League of Nations binding themselves to side against any Power which broke a treaty . . . or which refused, in case of dispute, to adopt some other method of settlement than that of war?"

Grey could not have put his questions to any person more likely to respond positively than Wilson. In mid-August 1914, he had said to Stockton Axson, his brother-in-law: "1. There must never again be a foot of ground acquired by conquest. 2. It must be recognized in fact that the small nations are on an equality of rights with the great nations. 3. Ammunition must be manufactured by governments and not by private individuals. 4. There must be some sort of an association of nations wherein all shall guarantee the territorial integrity of each." A few months later he began negotiations (unsuccessful, as it turned out, on account of Chile's opposition) for a Pan-American Pact to mutualize the Monroe Doctrine and bind the nations of the

New World in guarantees of the peaceful settlement of disputes and of territorial and political independence. The pact also provided for the governmental manufacture of armaments. Wilson was not acting unthinkingly, therefore, when he replied at once to Grey that the United States was prepared to join a league of nations and give the guarantees that Grey had demanded.

We have seen how Wilson, following the peaceful settlement of the *Sussex* controversy, took the public initiative in a move to implement the House-Grey plan by announcing, in his address to the League to Enforce Peace on May 27, 1916, that the United States was ready to join any feasible peacekeeping organization—as he put it, "an universal association of the nations to maintain the inviolate security of the highway of the seas for the common and unhindered use of all the nations of the world, and to prevent any war begun either contrary to treaty covenants or without warning and full submission of the causes to the opinion of the world—a virtual guarantee of territorial integrity and political independence."

Wilson was so encouraged by what seemed to be a nearly unanimous bipartisan approval of the league idea that he next incorporated a league plank into the Democratic platform of 1916 and made the league idea one of the chief features of his campaign speeches.

Wilson's third and most important step was to conjoin the league plan with the liberal peace program in his "Peace without Victory" speech of January 22, 1917. "I am proposing, as it were," he concluded, "that the nations should with one accord adopt the doctrine of President Monroe as the doctrine of the world: that no nation should seek to extend its polity over any other nation or people . . . that all nations henceforth avoid entangling alliances which would draw them into competitions of power."

On March 7, 1917, Wilson told the French Ambassador to the United States, Jean Jules Jusserand, that he was above all eager to see a "scientific" and just peace, one that would not create any new Alsace-Lorraines to endanger the future peace of the world. He said that he had no illusions about the league of nations to be formed. It would have to develop slowly. It would be necessary to begin with a universal entente, with the mutual obligation to submit international disputes to a conference of countries not directly involved. Perhaps that would, little by little, create precedents which would break the habit of the recourse to arms. It would be an experience to try.*

At about the same time, he set down for the guidance of the State Department what he called "Bases of Peace":

1. Mutual guarantee of political independence,—absolute in all domestic matters, limited in external affairs only by the rights of other nations.

2. Mutual guarantee of territorial integrity. NOTE: The application of this guarantee to the territorial arrangements made by the terms of the peace by which the present war is ended would, of course, necessarily depend upon the character of those arrangements, that is, their reasonableness and natural prospect of permanency; and would depend, so far as the participation of the United States is concerned, upon whether they were in conformity with the general principles of right and comity set forth in the address of the President of the Senate on the twenty-second of January last.

3. Mutual guarantee against such economic warfare as would in effect constitute an effort to throttle the industrial life of a nation or shut it off from equal opportunities of trade with the rest of the world. NOTE: This would, of course, not apply to any laws of any individual state which were meant merely for the regulation and development of its own industries or for the mere safeguarding of its own resources from misuse or exhaustion, but only to such legislation and such governmental action as could be shown to be intended to operate outside territorial limits and intended to injure particular rivals or groups of rivals.

4. Limitation of armaments, whether on land or sea, to the necessities of internal order and the probable demands of cooperation in making good the foregoing guarantees. (NOTE:) *Provided* the nations which take part in this covenant may be safely regarded as representing the major force of mankind.

GENERAL NOTE: It is suggested that it would not be necessary to set up at the outset any permanent tribunal or administrative agency, but only an Office of correspondence through which

---

*Wilson also told Jusserand that he had not meant to suggest the destruction of the Hapsburg Empire. That would not be desirable in any event. All that he had in mind was a grant of broad autonomy to the subject nationalities of the empire.

all matters of information could be cleared up, correspondence translated by experts (scholars), and mutual explanations and suggestions interchanged. It would in all likelihood be best to await the developments and suggestions of experience before attempting to set up any common instrumentality of international action.

Wilson's role and responsibilities of course changed drastically after the adoption of the war resolution. As the leader of one of the great belligerent powers he was now responsible for a massive mobilization of the country's entire resources for war. He was also responsible for all high-level negotiations with the Allied governments about shipping, supplies, the disposition and use of American ships and fighting men, and so on. Significantly, however, Wilson's supreme objective did not change. He had gone to war in order to wage peace. His objective, as he said in his war message, was still the attainment of a peace of justice and reconciliation. "Let us be very clear, and make clear to all the world what our motives and our objects are." He now had exactly the same things in mind as when he addressed the Senate on January 22 and the two houses on February 3 and 23. Moreover, Americans had no quarrel with the great German people, only feelings of sympathy and friendship.

Nor did Wilson's position change after American belligerency. He stood serenely above the passions and hatreds that rent Europe and were beginning to consume his own people as the one spokesman and leader of all peoples who desired a just and lasting peace. Wilson revealed his feelings in a hundred ways by what he thought, did, and said during the seventeen months of American belligerency.

First, he was careful to define America's peculiar role in the war. He had no desire to spare American resources and manpower, was prepared to continue the struggle to the bitter end if necessary, and strongly supported all proposals for closer Allied and American military cooperation. Yet he took assiduous pains to make it clear that the United States was in the war for its own reasons; and that it was fighting as an *associate,* not an ally, of the Entente powers.

This distinction reveals Wilson's fundamental thinking about the nature of the war and the role that the United States should play in it. He has often been misquoted as saying that the war was one for democracy; actually, he said that it was a war to make the world *safe* for democracy. He never deluded himself into thinking that the United States and the Allies were fighting for the same objectives. He probably did not know all the details of the Allied secret treaties for the division of enemy territories and colonies.* But he knew many of their important terms. The main terms of the Treaty of London, under which Italy entered the war, were published in the *New York Times* a week after the treaty was signed. Moreover, the reply that the Allies

---

*This brings up the question of whether Wilson lied to the Senate Foreign Relations Committee in 1919 when he said that he had not seen these secret treaties before he went to Paris. Arthur Balfour sent him copies of them on May 18, 1917; Wilson acknowledged receipt of them one day later; and the copies are still in his papers. Thomas A. Bailey has concluded in *Woodrow Wilson and the Lost Peace* (1944), pp. 147–48, that Wilson probably lied to the Foreign Relations Committee for political purposes. Wilson was not in the habit of lying, however, and it is almost inconceivable that he would have deliberately lied to so important a committee. First, Wilson would not have gained anything politically by lying; on the contrary, he might have earned some political credit by saying that of course he had read the secret treaties, and that they had created some of his main problems at Paris. Second, there is no evidence in the Wilson Papers or the State Department archives of any reference in memoranda or correspondence to the secret treaties. Third, the executive committee of The Inquiry, on about January 2, 1918, submitted a long memorandum to Wilson on suggested peace terms. In this careful review of Allied claims, there is not a single reference to any of the Allied secret treaties. Fourth, Wilson told his physician, Dr. Cary T. Grayson, during the peace conference that, every time it seemed that he was about to make progress on a difficult issue, one of the spokesmen of the great Allied powers would come up with a secret treaty that he, Wilson, had not heard of.

Wilson usually marked up the important documents that he read—by underscoring sentences, drawing vertical lines alongside paragraphs, or making marginal comments. The copies of the treaties in the Wilson Papers bear no signs that Wilson had read them.

What seems most likely is the following: On April 28, 1917, Balfour and House talked in a general way about peace terms and, more particularly, about some of the secret arrangements that the Allies had made among themselves, especially the Treaty of London. Wilson, House, and Balfour had a long conversation at the White House on April 30. Wilson did much of the talking, but House finally steered the conversation around to the problem of the secret treaties. How many details Balfour divulged, we do not know. However, it is clear from Balfour's letter to Wilson of May 18, 1917, that Wilson said that he did not consider the United States bound by any secret Allied arrangements. He probably added that he was not interested in them. "I do not think that they will add much to the knowledge which you already possess of our negotiations since the War began," Balfour wrote, *"nor do I think they are likely to modify your general views"* (emphasis mine).

It would seem a reasonable conclusion, in the light of the foregoing, that Wilson filed the treaties that Balfour sent without reading them.

sent to Wilson on January 10, 1917, was explicit and detailed. However all this may have been, Wilson jealously guarded his freedom of action, first, by refusing to discuss peace terms with any Allied leader during the early months of the war and, second, by making it unmistakably clear in his public addresses all through the war what his, or the American, terms would be.

Wilson pressed his campaign for peace with mounting intensity as the months passed in 1917. First, he applied heavy pressure on Austria-Hungary to withdraw from the war. He promised that the American and the Allied governments would insist only upon a federalization, and not the destruction, of that empire. More important, he tried to make it clear to the German people that they could have peace on generous terms at any time, provided only that they depose their military masters, repudiate aims of conquest and world dominion, and withdraw their armies from the conquered territories. Again and again, he said that Americans had no quarrel with the great German people, admired their accomplishments, and, above all, coveted their friendship.

"We intend no wrong against the German Empire," Wilson said, for example, on December 4, 1917,

> no interference with her internal affairs. We should deem either the one or the other absolutely unjustifiable, absolutely contrary to the principles we have professed to live by and to hold most sacred throughout our life as a nation. The people of Germany are being told by the men whom they now permit to deceive them and to act as their masters that they are fighting for the very life and existence of their Empire, a war of desperate self-defense against deliberate aggression. Nothing could be more grossly or wantonly false. . . . We are in fact fighting for their emancipation from fear, along with our own—from the fear as well as from the fact of unjust attack by neighbors or rivals or schemers after world empire. No one is threatening the existence or the independence or the peaceful enterprise of the German Empire.

There was much truth in a British contemporary's quip that Wilson was talking more like a mediator than a belligerent. He certainly hoped all through 1917 that the moderate forces in the Reichstag (the German parliament) and the civilian leaders in the Imperial government would take control from the High Command and appeal for a peace conference. Wilson correctly regarded the Kaiser as a figurehead of the military. Had such a turnover of power occurred in Berlin, then Wilson almost certainly would have responded eagerly, even if Allied refusal to cooperate had resulted in a separate peace between the United States and Germany.

Wilson had no fears of any such rupture with the Allies. He had great faith in his own ability to marshal world opinion behind a generous settlement. As he warned in his address of December 4, 1917:

> Statesmen must by this time have learned that the opinion of the world is everywhere wide awake and fully comprehends the issues involved. No representative of any self-governed nation will dare disregard it by attempting any . . . covenants of selfishness and compromise. . . . The congress that concludes this war will feel the full strength of the tide that runs now in the hearts of consciences of free men everywhere.

There was, besides, the reassuring fact that the Allies were absolutely dependent economically and were growing militarily dependent upon the United States. Indeed, no one could foresee victory on the western front without a large American army to break the stalemate in the trenches. This meant, as Wilson wrote to Colonel House in July 1917, "When the war is over we can force them to our way of thinking, because by that time they [the Allies] will, among other things, be financially in our hands."

Growing confidence in his own power and leadership, evidence of war weariness everywhere in Europe (mutinies broke out in sixteen corps of the French army in the spring of 1917), and signs of revolt in the Reichstag against the High Command (the Reichstag adopted a no-annexation, no-indemnities resolution on July 19, 1917) all stimulated in Wilson the desire to strike for peace in some dramatic way.

Wilson was strongly tempted to respond clearly when Pope Benedict XV, on August 1, 1917, called for peace on a basis of the evacuation of conquered territories, mutual reparation, and a settlement of territorial questions in accord, insofar as possible, with the wishes of the peoples involved. Perhaps Wilson resented Benedict's taking the initiative, and there was good evidence that the Pope was under strong Austrian influence. There were other reasons why Wilson did not respond more positively to Benedict. Wilson had not had time to confer with the Allied governments and feared that such discussions would only provoke dissenting voices from France and Italy, because the United States was not interested in their territorial claims. Wilson also had not had the time himself to concentrate on a detailed plan for peace. Whatever the real reason, Wilson answered the Pope only in general terms. He said that the American people had no desire for "punitive damages, the dismemberment of empires, the establishment of selfish and exclusive economic leagues." He also warned that no enduring peace could be made until the German military imperialists had been deposed.

Nonetheless, the Pope's initiative did strongly stimulate Wilson's desire to move for peace. "My own feeling," he wrote to House on August 23, "is that we should speak at the earliest possible moment now." Wilson wasted no time from this point on in preparing for a climactic drive for peace. First, on September 2, he asked House to assemble a group of experts, subsequently called The Inquiry to study the war aims of all the belligerents and advise him on the specifics of an American peace program. Next, late in October, Wilson sent House to London and Paris to participate in inter-Allied military discussions and, incidentally, to press for agreement on war aims.

The opportunity, indeed the necessity, for a peace move came almost as soon as House arrived in London. The Bolsheviks seized control of the Russian government on November 7 and appealed to the Allies to begin negotiations at once looking toward a peace based upon the principles of no annexations and no indemnities. Now in Paris, House pleaded with the British and French leaders to approve a preliminary reply in the form of a simple announcement of liberal war aims. That, House urged, might at least persuade the Bolshevik authorities to try to maintain the Russian war effort. Wilson sent the stern warnings that the American people would not fight for "any selfish aim on the part of any belligerent," and that it would be a "fatal mistake" for the Allies "to cool the ardour of America." The British and French were adamant. They would not even approve an innocuous declaration of war aims. House returned empty-handed to Washington in mid-December.

Events of the next two weeks convinced Wilson that he himself would have to make an authoritative statement. The Bolsheviks signed a separate armistice with the Central Powers on December 15 and appealed for the assembling of a *general* peace conference at once. The new Russian leaders also published the secret treaties between the czarist government and the Allies negotiated since the beginning of the war; they pointed to the refusal of the Entente powers to join a peace conference as proof of their perfidious ambitions. Czernin, the Austrian Foreign Minister, speaking on Christmas Day, echoed the Bolshevik appeal and declared that the Central Powers desired no forcible annexations, would deprive no country of its independence, and wanted minorities to enjoy the right of self-determination. Liberals, idealists, labor leaders, and Socialists in the United States and Great Britain were excited. They denounced Allied intransigence, declared that the time for peace had come, and demanded that a frank reply be sent to the Russian and Austrian overtures.

It was in these circumstances that Wilson set to work with Colonel House on January 4, 1918, on what was to become the Fourteen Points Address. With a long memorandum prepared by the executive committee of The Inquiry as a guide, he hammered out on his own typewriter a statement intended to appeal to German and Austrian moderates, to reply to the Bolsheviks, and, above all, to make clear to all the world the aspirations and ideals for which the American people were fighting.

The address was completed on January 7, and Wilson read it to a joint session of Congress on the following day. He began by reviewing events that had occurred in Russia only a few days before—the disruption of the negotiations at Brest-Litovsk between the Russian and German-Austrian negotiators following the presentation of extraordinarily severe demands by the German delegation. It was evident, Wilson said, that the German military masters were bent upon the conquest and subjugation of the helpless Russian people. Therefore, the time had come for the peace-loving nations to avow their ideals and objectives, and these he summarized in fourteen points.

On the one hand there were the general points promising open diplomacy, openly arrived at; absolute freedom of the seas in peace and war alike, "except as the seas may be closed in whole or in part by international action for the enforcement of international covenants"; limitation of armaments to the lowest level consistent with domestic safety; the removal, insofar as possible, of barriers to international trade; an absolutely impartial and open-minded settlement of colonial claims, with due regard given to the interests of the people involved; and the establishment of a league of nations to protect great and small states alike.

On the other hand there were the points relating to specific issues. Two of these—the evacuation and restoration of Belgium and the evacuation of Russia and the self-determination of the Russian people—were, like the general points, indispensable to a peace settlement. The remaining six points were not quite as important, for in defining them Wilson said that they "should" rather than "must" be achieved. They were, presumably, negotiable. They were the return of Alsace-Lorraine to France. Wilson had great difficulty in framing this point—the chief French war objective—and in deciding whether to include it. House wanted him to leave it out altogether! The other five were autonomy for the subject peoples of the Austro-Hungarian Empire; a readjustment of Italy's boundary along clearly recognizable lines of nationality; the evacuation of the Balkans and free development for the states of that region; security for the Turkish portions of the Ottoman Empire, but autonomy for the subject peoples of that empire and internationalization of the Dardanelles; and the creation of an independent Polish state with access to the sea and international guarantees of its independence.

There was an implied fifteenth point, one as important as any of the fourteen—that the United States had no jealousy of Germany's greatness and no desire to do her any injury. As he put it:

> We grudge her no achievement or distinction of learning or of pacific enterprise such as have made her record very bright and very enviable. We do not wish to injure her or to block in any way her legitimate influence of power. We do not wish to fight her either with arms or with hostile arrangements of trade if she

is willing to associate herself with us and the other peace-loving nations of the world in covenants of justice and law and fair dealing. We wish her only to accept a place of equality among the peoples of the world,—the new world in which we now live, —instead of a place of mastery.

The final paragraphs clearly implied that the United States would be willing to go at once to the peace table if the Germans would accept the fourteen points as the basis for a settlement. It was not even necessary, Wilson said, for the Germans to alter their political institutions. But it was necessary for the United States to know who spoke for Germany—the majority of the Reichstag, or the military party whose creed was domination. The moral climax of the war had now come, and the American people were ready for the test. Germany, Wilson was saying, could obtain a generous settlement if she wanted one.

It would be almost superfluous to remark upon the impact and importance of the Fourteen Points Address. It immediately became the moral standard to which liberals, labor leaders, and Socialists in the United States and Europe rallied. British Labourites hailed Wilson as their own spokesman. The entire French Left, as one authority has written, were "galvanized into the President's most ardent supporter in the Entente." Even V. I. Lenin, head of the Bolshevik government, warmly responded that the address was "a potential agency promoting peace"; the address was printed in *Izvestiya,* the official Bolshevik daily, and distributed widely throughout Russia.

For a time it seemed that Wilson had begun transatlantic conversations that might lead to an armistice and peace negotiations. Czernin responded in an address to the Foreign Affairs Committee of the Austrian Reichsrath on January 24. He said that the Austro-Hungarian government agreed for the most part with Wilson, and that the fourteen points provided an acceptable basis for peace negotiations. The new German Chancellor, Count Georg F. von Hertling, gave his reply in an address to the Main Committee of the Reichstag on the same day that Czernin spoke. Germany, he said, could certainly agree with many of the President's general points, but it would brook no interference in its negotiations with Russia. Hertling was evasive about Belgium, and said that Germany would never return Alsace-Lorraine to France.

Wilson answered them in an address to a joint session of Congress on February 11. He commended Czernin's moderation and declared that Hertling's speech had been double-talk to mask the ambitions of Germany's military leaders. Peace, he said, could not be made by old methods and according to old standards. National aspirations had to be respected, for self-determination was the new rule of international life. The question of whether peace conversations could continue, he concluded, depended upon agreement on four principles: justice should govern the settlement of all issues; peoples should not be bartered and sold in the discredited game of balance of power; every territorial settlement should be made *for the benefit of the peoples involved;* and all well-defined national aspirations should be accorded satisfaction insofar as possible.

This brief transatlantic dialogue came to an abrupt end on March 3, 1918, when the Germans imposed a Carthaginian peace upon the Russians at Brest-Litovsk. Wilson expressed his disillusionment and despair in a speech at Baltimore on April 6. He had tried, he said, to judge Germany's purposes without hatred or vindictiveness. He still believed that the German civilian leaders wanted a peace of justice. However, the Treaty of Brest-Litovsk had revealed that Germany's real masters sought the domination of Europe. Almost in anguish, he cried out that there was only one response that the American people could give: "Force, Force to the utmost, Force without stint or limit, the righteous and triumphant Force which shall make Right the law of the world, and cast every selfish dominion down in the dust."

The poignancy of Wilson's consternation at the Treaty of Brest-Litovsk becomes clearer when one recalls what that treaty portended. It meant that peace could be won only by smashing the power of the German military machine. This, in turn, meant a settlement, not negotiated among equals, but imposed by the victors—in short a situation of grave difficulty for the man who knew that it would be as necessary to restrain the ambitions of his associates as to defeat those of his enemies. But peace without victory was no longer possible after March 1918. With Russia prostrate, the German High Command decided to go for all-out victory on the western front. It transferred some forty divisions from the eastern front and launched a gigantic offensive to knock France out of the war before the trickle of American reinforcements could become a mighty stream. The French and British forces reeled and retreated under the heavy blows. "The Past and Present are in deadly grapple," Wilson cried out on July 4, "and the peoples of the world are being done to death between them. There can be but one issue. The settlement must be final. There can be no compromise. . . . No halfway decision is conceivable."

The French defenses held before Paris in mid-July. Soon afterward, with the help of an ever-growing American Expeditionary Force, the supreme Allied commander, Marshal Ferdinand Foch, began a counteroffensive. By October 1, the combined Allied and American armies had broken the Hindenburg Line and were nearing the Belgian and German frontiers. Panic-stricken, General Erich von Ludendorff then demanded that the Imperial government obtain an immediate armistice in order to give him time to withdraw his armies to new defensive positions.

The German government responded by appealing to Wilson, *not* to the Allied governments, for an armistice on the basis of the Fourteen Points and Wilson's subsequent war addresses.* Wilson was not taken in by the German leaders. He deftly maneuvered them into

*These included the Four Supplementary points of February 11, 1918, the Four Additional Points of July 4, 1918, and the Five Additional Points of September 27, 1918.

I have enumerated the Four Supplementary Points of February 11 in the body of the text above. The Four Additional Points of July 4 were the destruction or reduction to virtual impotence of every arbitrary power anywhere that could disturb the peace of the world, *e.g.*, the German military establishment; the settlement of every question upon the basis of the free acceptance of that settlement by the people immediately concerned; the consent of all nations to be governed in their conduct toward each other by the same principles of honor and of respect for law that governed the individual citizens of all modern states in their relations with one another; and the establishment of a peace organization that would "make it certain that the combined power of free nations will check every invasion of right and serve to make peace and justice . . . secure."

The Five Additional Points of September 27 were that equal justice should be done to all peoples in the peace settlement; that special interests should not be permitted to override the common interest; that there should be no special understandings within the general family of the league of nations; that there should be no selfish economic combinations or any form of economic coercion within the league, except as a means of preventing aggression; and that all international agreements should be made known in their entirety to the rest of the world.

acknowledgement of defeat and agreement to accept an armistice that would render them powerless to resume *offensive* operations. However, he wanted to maintain enough German power to serve as a counterbalance to Allied might. "It is certain," he advised Colonel House on October 28, "that too much success or security on the part of the Allies will make a genuine peace settlement exceedingly difficult, if not impossible." This required an armistice agreement that left the German ground forces intact, one which, as he put it, "would prevent a renewal of hostilities by Germany but which will be as moderate and reasonable as possible within those limits."

Wilson's decision to go forward with armistice negotiations carried heavy risks at home and abroad. In the United States, Theodore Roosevelt led the chorus demanding a drive to Berlin and a dictated peace. Abroad, the Allies were naturally reluctant to promise Germany to make peace upon a basis of the fourteen points and Wilson's later pronouncements, when total victory was so near.

Determined to end the bloodshed, Wilson sent Colonel House to Paris in mid-October to force a final showdown before the collapse of German resistance had emboldened the Allied leaders into taking peace negotiations into their own hands. From October 29 through November 4, House confronted the Allied prime ministers in a series of stormy meetings. When they threatened to repudiate the fourteen points, House countered with the warning that Wilson was prepared to make a separate peace. The result was an agreement to promise Germany terms as stipulated in the Fourteen Points Address and Wilson's subsequent declarations, amended only by a British reservation concerning the point relating to freedom of the seas and a French "elucidation" providing that Germany should be required to make compensation for the civilian damages caused by her aggressions.

House, in a telegram to Wilson on November 5, boasted of his "great diplomatic victory," and so it was in a sense. However, Foch, aided by General John J. Pershing, head of the A.E.F. and a hardliner, imposed such military and naval terms, most importantly, French occupation of the Rhineland and the internment of the German navy, as to put Germany completely at the mercy of the British and French. Thus the armistice signed on November 11 was a shadow victory for House and a substantive victory for the Allies, particularly

France. Although Wilson had questioned the necessity of occupying Alsace-Lorraine and opposed the occupation of the Rhineland, now he had no alternative but to accept the package that was known as the Pre-Armistice Agreement.

The opportunity for which Wilson had waited since 1914 was now almost at hand. In spite of some advice to the contrary, he had decided to go to Paris as the head of the American delegation, on the commonsense ground that the peace conference would be a summit meeting, and that only he could meet other heads of government on equal ground. No leader in history ever embarked upon a fateful undertaking with higher hopes or nobler ambitions. However, his bargaining position had been additionally weakened by the time he sailed for France on December 4, 1918. On October 25, he had made a frankly partisan appeal for the election of a Democratic Congress and had said that a Republican victory "would . . . certainly be interpreted on the other side of the water as a repudiation of my leadership." Republicans had won both houses of Congress, and their leaders were now saying that Wilson did not represent the American people on his fateful mission to France. Second, all of western Europe was in a state of nearly psychotic shock after more than four years of bloodletting. Passions of hatred and revenge were surging through the British, French, and Italian peoples and inevitably infected their spokesmen. These primeval forces, beyond Wilson's control, boded ill for one who wanted only to do what was right and just. Among other things, his suggestion that Germany be represented at the peace conference was rejected peremptorily.

The first stage of the Paris Peace Conference began when it opened on January 18, 1919, and ended when Wilson left for a visit to the United States on February 14. Two main issues—relations with the Bolshevik regime and creation of a league of nations—dominated the discussions. The second stage lasted from Wilson's departure to his return to Paris on March 14. During this period, Colonel House, designated by Wilson as his spokesman, betrayed Wilson in violation of explicit instructions by consenting to "speed up" the conference by agreement upon a "preliminary" peace treaty. It provided, among other things, for punitive military terms, the establishment of a

French-controlled Republic of the Rhine, and the scuttling, at least for a time, of the League of Nations. The third stage lasted from March 24 until about May 7, when agreement on a treaty with Germany was reached. During this period, Wilson had his hardest struggles and made his most important compromises.* The final stage lasted from May 7, when the Treaty was presented to the German delegation, to June 28, when it was signed in the Hall of Mirrors at Versailles. During this period, Wilson and his colleagues responded to the German protests against the Treaty presented on May 7 and made some important changes in response.

The overshadowing issue of the Paris Peace Conference was security for France against future German aggression. Wilson offered security in a Reich that was reformed because now democratic, and in the League of Nations that would provide machinery to prevent future German aggression. Such assurances were not enough for the French. Their territory had been invaded twice by Germany in less than half a century; France was still, in 1919, inferior in manpower, resources, and industry to Germany. The French were determined to destroy the German colossus once and for all and to guarantee their safety in the future. Thus Clemenceau followed plans devised by Marshal Foch and approved even before the United States had entered the war. These included, in addition to the recovery of Alsace-

---

*Wilson made these compromises, which will be discussed later, in early April, during the last stages of and immediately following a severe attack of influenza and encephalitis. Dr. Edwin A. Weinstein, who is writing a medical biography of Wilson, has suggested that Wilson may have been experiencing the euphoria that often accompanies recovery from encephalitis and hence may not have been acting with his characteristic resolution. Dr. Weinstein points to Wilson's quick acquiescence in a provision for the trial of the Kaiser for war crimes, which Wilson had heretofore strongly opposed.

Dr. Weinstein may well be correct. However, this was the period when the confrontation between Wilson and Georges Clemenceau, the French Premier, reached its peak. There was serious danger that Wilson would go home and disrupt the conference. Compromise with Clemenceau was the only alternative to this disaster, and Wilson might well have deliberately chosen the way of compromise. He might also have thought that the provision for the trial of the Kaiser, which he thought ridiculous, would never be carried out, as, indeed, it was not.

Incidentally, the cause of Wilson's loss of confidence in Colonel House was House's behavior during Wilson's absence, not the concessions of early April, which some historians have inaccurately attributed to House.

Lorraine, tearing the west bank of the Rhine from Germany and the establishment of one or more autonomous Rhenish republics under French control.

Wilson opposed this plan with grim determination. He argued that the dismemberment of Germany in the West would outrageously violate the Pre-Armistice Agreement and create a wound that would fester until it produced another war. The tension reached its climax during late March and early April. Clemenceau accused Wilson of being pro-German; Wilson ordered his ship to raise steam and be prepared to take him back to the United States.

Compromise was the only alternative to the disruption of the conference. In the showdown, it was Clemenceau who made the vital concession—by yielding his demand for the creation of the Rhenish republics and permanent French occupation of the Rhineland. In return, Wilson and David Lloyd George, the British Prime Minister (who gave Wilson indispensable support at this juncture), agreed to permit a fifteen-year occupation of the Rhineland and signed with Clemenceau treaties promising that, for a limited period, the United States and Great Britain would come to France's aid if she was attacked by Germany. These were reasonable concessions, and they saved the conference from disruption. Further to assure French security—and these were non-controversial provisions—Wilson and the Allied leaders agreed on the permanent demilitarization of the west bank of the Rhine and a strip along the east bank, and on severe limitations on German military forces of all categories.

The issue of reparations and indemnities provoked the most protracted debates at the conference and the greatest bitterness in Germany afterward. In cynical disregard of the Pre-Armistice Agreement, which strongly implied that Germany should be liable only for civilian damages, Clemenceau and Lloyd George, under heavy pressure from their own peoples, demanded that Germany be made to shoulder the entire costs of the war to the Allied peoples as well as its partial costs to their governments. Wilson made his most important concessions at Paris on this issue. First, he agreed that Germany should be forced to bear the costs of disability pensions to Allied veterans and their families, on the ground that these were really civilian damages. Second, he agreed that the French should have the right to occupy the Rhineland if the Germans failed to meet their reparations obligations. The French demanded ownership of the Saar Valley in compensation for the wanton destruction wrought in France by the retreating German armies. Wilson fought this demand bitterly and successfully on the ground that the Saar was German territory. However, he did agree to French ownership of the Saar coal mines and French administration of the territory for fifteen years under the supervision of the League of Nations. At the end of this period, the inhabitants of the Valley should vote whether to remain under French jurisdiction or to return to Germany. In addition, Wilson consented to the immediate seizure of some $5 billion worth of German property. Finally, Wilson agreed to the inclusion of the much-controverted Article 231 in the treaty, by which Germany and her allies acknowledged legal responsibility for all losses incurred during the war by the Allied peoples and governments. Responsibility under the article actually was limited to civilian damages covered by Article 232, and Article 231 was inserted to provide a legal basis for reparations demands and not, as historians later thought, to force Germany to acknowledge entire guilt for the war.

Meanwhile, Wilson, with the strong support of his economic advisers, had been fighting hard for a project that would have made all the controversy over reparations so much shadowboxing. It was to establish a Reparations Commission instructed to set a fixed schedule of payments to be made for *a definite period,* and also instructed to determine the total sum of reparations upon the basis of Germany's *capacity to pay.* The pressure from the French was so heavy that Wilson, on April 5, surrendered unconditionally and agreed that the Reparations Commission should be instructed only to compute the reparations bill and to enforce its complete payment, without any reference to a definite period of capacity to pay.

Perhaps Wilson made this, his most important concession at the conference, in the conviction that it would not matter much in the long run. He knew that the Allies would never be able to collect the astronomical sums that they expected. He knew that the Allies could not collect huge sums without bankrupting the German economy, the well being of which was absolutely essential to the prosperity of western Europe. He also knew that passions would eventually cool.

And he must have thought that the Reparations Commission, under American leadership, would gradually handle the reparations problem in a sensible and realistic way. This, in fact, is what did occur in the 1920s with the establishment of the Dawes and Young commissions of 1923–1924 and 1929. Finally, in 1932, the European powers, meeting in Lausanne, Switzerland, ended the problem altogether. They reduced Germany's obligations to some $700 million and tacitly acknowledged that this sum would never have to be paid.

A third issue was the question of the disposition of the former German colonies in Africa, the Pacific area, and the Far East, all of which had been captured by Allied forces during the war. In the Fourteen Points Address, Wilson had called for an "absolutely impartial adjustment of all colonial claims," with due regard for the interests of the peoples involved. He explained what he had in mind during preconference discussions in London in December 1918. It was to make the former German colonies the common property of the League of Nations and to have them governed by small nations under specific international mandate and supervision. At no time did Wilson contemplate the return of the colonies to Germany, for he agreed with the experts who told him that the Germans had been oppressive and exploitative masters—an opinion, incidentally, still held by specialists in the field of colonial administration. The main obstacle to Wilson's plan were the commitments that the British government had made to the dominions and the Allied governments to Japan.

The issue was fought out during the early days of the conference, with Wilson arrayed *alone* against Lloyd George and the representatives of the dominions and Japan. There was no way that Wilson could have won a clear-cut victory, so adamant were the dominions and Japan that British commitments and Allied treaty promises be honored. Wilson, moreover, soon abandoned his plan for mandating the colonies to small nations on the ground that it was impractical and accepted the necessity of a division on the basis of occupation. But he refused to yield his chief objective—the clear establishment of the principle that the governments to which the former German colonies were awarded would administer them under the specific mandate of the League of Nations and for the benefit of the native peoples and of the entire world. This he achieved in the mandate system established by the Covenant of the League of Nations.

Wilson suffered momentary defeat on the closely related issue of Japanese rights in Shantung Province of China, a matter much more complicated than the disposition of the German colonies because it involved what Wilson thought were moral principles and the right of the Chinese to control their own territory. The Japanese had entered the war in 1914, captured the German naval base at Kiaochow, and overrun the entire German concession in Shantung Province. Afterward, from 1915 to 1917, they had imposed treaties upon the Chinese government recognizing their rights as Germany's successors in the province. They had also won similar recognition from the foreign offices in London, Paris, and Petrograd. Legally, the Japanese claims at Paris to control of Shantung Province were impregnable.

Legal (or treaty) rights carried little weight with the man who was determined to help the Chinese government recover a lost province. Wilson set out to vindicate the principle of self-determination with almost incredible vigor and courage. When he could win no support from the European leaders, he personally brought the Chinese delegates before the conference so that they might plead their own case. He appealed to sentiments and principles with great eloquence and urged the Japanese to make their contribution to a better world by foregoing conquest. He yielded only because the Japanese warned that they would not sign the Treaty and join the League of Nations if they were forced to evacuate Shantung Province immediately. However, Wilson did win verbal promises from the Japanese government that it would restore full political sovereignty to China in the near future. The Japanese honored this pledge in 1922.

Italian claims to former parts of the Austro-Hungarian Empire provoked the bitterest personal acrimony and the longest dispute at the Paris Peace Conference. Italy had entered the war on the Allied side in 1915 under the terms of the Treaty of London, which promised Italy the Austrian Trentino to the Brenner Pass, the district of Trieste, the Dalmatian coast south of the port of Fiume, and other territories.

There would have been great conflict between Wilson and the Italians at Paris over this matter if the latter had been able to keep their appetite for territory within reasonable bounds. Wilson followed the interpretation of the Fourteen Points prepared by Frank I. Cobb and Walter Lippmann of The Inquiry in October 1918 and conceded Italy's claim to the Trentino on strategic grounds even before the peace conference opened. (He probably regretted this concession once he realized how much it violated the principle of self-determination.) Nor did he object to Italian claims to Trieste, occupied largely by Italians, which were in accord with the principle of self-determination.

Fur began to fly when Italian Prime Minister Vittorio Orlando and Foreign Minister Sidney Sonnino demanded also Fiume, which had been awarded to the South Slavs by the Treaty of London and would be the only good outlet to the sea for the new state of Yugoslavia. This alienated Lloyd George and Clemenceau and gave Wilson a strategic opportunity that he quickly exploited: He capitalized on the Italian claim to Fiume to justify a sweeping denial of the Italian claim to the Dalmatian coast on the ground that possesssion of it was essential to Yugoslav national security.

The climax of the grueling battle came on April 23. Wilson, weary of making futile pleas to master practitioners of the old diplomacy, appealed over their heads to the Italian people. Orlando and Sonnino left the conference in a huff, but they returned in early May after it was evident that Wilson would not yield. The matter never was resolved at Paris. It was left for settlement by the League of Nations and by direct negotiations between Italy and Yugoslavia.

Four other great issues before the Paris Peace Conference were only slightly less important than the ones just discussed. The easiest problem was the creation of an independent Polish state. All the belligerents had promised during the war to establish some kind of an autonomous Poland. The rebirth of a truly independent Poland, that is, one not under the control either of Russia or of Germany and Austria-Hungary, was one of Wilson's principal peace objectives at least since his "Peace without Victory" speech. The only controversies of any consequence over Poland involved the disposition of the port of Danzig—Poland's "access to the sea"—and the division of the German province of Upper Silesia. In both disputes, Wilson and Lloyd George stood firm against Polish and French extreme demands. They won the establishment of Danzig as a free port under the jurisdiction of the League of Nations, secure transit rights for Germany to East Prussia, and a plebiscite to determine the partitioning of Upper Silesia between Germany and Poland.

Second, it was necessary to decide the fate of the remains of the Austro-Hungarian Empire. Wilson's role in this matter has been gravely misunderstood and distorted, especially by British critics who have imputed to him virtually entire responsibility for the destruction of the empire and the Balkanization of central Europe. This is an exaggeration worthy of the good Baron Münchausen. Before the summer of 1918, Wilson had asked for the federalization, not the breakup, of the Hapsburg realm. The Austro-Hungarian Empire had already fallen apart from within before Wilson specifically amended the fourteen points by recognizing the new state of Czechoslovakia, and in doing so he was simply following the lead of the British and French governments. The new states of Central Europe existed in fact by the time that the Paris Peace Conference met. They would have been recognized as independent states even if Wilson had never uttered the word "self-determination." All that Wilson, or anyone else at Paris, for that matter, could do was to try to draw the least absurd boundaries possible. However, Wilson did insist upon and obtain provisions aimed at preserving the economic unity of the area, like the internationalization of the Danube, and protecting minorities in the successor states.

There has been even greater misunderstanding (some of it concocted for political purposes) about Wilson's attitude and policies toward the Bolshevik regime, a third major problem. The situation in Russia constantly changed, and it was usually impossible to know what was really happening there on account of conflicting reports. Through all the chaos, however, Wilson acted as consistently as possible on five fundamental convictions.

The first was that the territorial integrity of the former Russian Empire had to be preserved, except for the detachment of the Polish territories in order to create the new Polish state.

Second, the Bolshevik Revolution was the result of centuries of oppression and exploitation of peasants and workers—an authentic social and economic revolution and an answer to egregious wrongs.

Third, the Russians could be dealt with only by attempting to help them remove the root causes of the revolution through relief and assistance.

Fourth, it would be futile and wrong to attempt to overthrow the

Bolshevik government by force. As Wilson said in Paris, "In my opinion, trying to stop a revolutionary movement by troops in the field is like using a broom to hold back a great ocean."

Fifth, and most important, the Russian people had the same right to self-determination as any other people. That is, they had the right to solve their own problems and hew out their own destiny with no outside interference. He stated this conviction most eloquently in the so-called Prinkipo Proposal (an invitation to the warring groups in Russia to send delegations to Paris), which he himself wrote, as follows:

> The single object the representatives of the associated Powers have had in mind in their discussions of the course they should pursue with regard to Russia has been to help the Russian people, not to hinder them, or to interfere in any manner with their right to settle their own affairs in their own way. They regard the Russian people as their friends not their enemies, and are willing to help them in any way they are willing to be helped. . . .
>
> They recognise the absolute right of the Russian people to direct their own affairs without dictation or direction of any kind from outside. They do not wish to exploit or make use of Russia in any way. They recognise the revolution without reservation, and will in no way, and in no circumstances, aid or give countenance to any attempt at a counter-revolution. It is not their wish or purpose to favour or assist any one of those organized groups now contending for the leadership and guidance of Russia as against the others. Their sole and sincere purpose is to do what they can to bring Russia peace and an opportunity to find her way out of her present troubles.

In accord with these convictions and sentiments, Wilson resisted heavy British and French pressure for what would have been an impossible effort to reestablish the eastern front during 1918. He finally yielded to what seemed to be military and humane necessities and, in the summer of 1918, sent a force of some 20,000 men under General William S. Graves to Vladivostok. Wilson took this action in order to keep open the door of escape for a sizable Czech army fleeing eastward from the Bolsheviks and also to keep an eye on the Japanese, who sent some 73,000 men to Siberia. He ordered General Graves to avoid all interference in internal Russian affairs, and Graves obeyed his orders strictly. Wilson also sent a force of some 15,500 men to Murmansk to help a small British detachment guard military supplies in Murmansk and Archangel against possible German capture. He gave strict orders to the commander of the American force to avoid any participation in the Russian Civil War. For some reason still unknown, these orders were delayed in transmission. By the time that they had reached Murmansk, American troops, acting under orders of a British officer, General F. C. Poole, who outranked the officer commanding the American contingent, Colonel George E. Stewart, were involved in fighting Bolshevik troops. Wilson received news of the fighting in Paris. He at once ordered the withdrawal of the American contingent as soon as weather conditions permitted. This, then, was the extent of American "intervention" in the Russian Civil War.

Ironically—in light of what certain so-called New Left American historians have written—Wilson was the one person who prevented large-scale military intervention in Russia. Virtually single-handedly, he foiled Marshall Foch's proposal for a Vienna-based "Grand Crusade," or military campaign, against Bolshevism, which had strong support in certain British quarters. The British and the French executed their own military interventions at this time and later, but Wilson was in no way responsible for these fiascos.

The fourth large problem was disarmament, the key, Wilson believed, to peace and security in the future. Wilson proposed that the victors accept virtually the same limitations on ground forces that they were imposing upon the Germans and agree in the peace treaty itself to abolish conscription, prohibit private manufacture of the implements of war, and maintain armies sufficient only to preserve domestic order and fulfill international obligations. He encountered insuperable opposition from the French and won only a vague promise to undertake general disarmament in the future. He did not propose to restrict navies because, for one reason, he was forced to use the threat of American naval expansion as a bargaining tool to win British support for the League of Nations. He was also deeply suspicious of Japanese imperialism and did not want to weaken the chief potential deterrent to Japanese ambitions.

The issue that took precedence over all the others in Wilson's plans and purposes—the question of the League of Nations—is mentioned last because it was so pervasively involved in all the discussions at Paris. There were two divergent concepts of what the League should be and do, and they cast a revealing light upon the motives and objectives of the opposing forces at Paris. One was the French concept of a league of victors, which would be used to guarantee French military domination of the Continent. The French plan was embodied in a draft presented at the first meeting of the League of Nations Commission on February 3, 1919. It envisaged the creation of an international army and a general staff with startling supranational powers, not unlike those later given to NATO. The other was Wilson's concept of a league of *all* nations, the vanquished as well as the victors—a universal alliance for the purpose of creating a concert of power, not really a supranational agency, but one depending upon the leadership of the great powers, the cooperation of sovereign states, and the organized opinion of mankind for its effectiveness.

As chairman and with strong British support, Wilson controlled the meetings of the commission that drafted the Covenant, or constitution, of the League. The crucial conflicts came when the French, Italians, Japanese, and even the British at times, ruthlessly threatened to refuse to support Wilson's league in order to exact concessions on other issues. Time and again Wilson did retreat, but by thus yielding he won the larger goal—a League of Nations constructed almost exactly as he wanted it.

The Covenant of the League was firmly embedded in all the treaties signed at Paris; it bound its signatory members in an alliance of nonaggression and friendship; and it created the machinery for international cooperation in many fields and for the prevention of war. The heart of the Covenant was embodied in Article 10, which read as follows:

> The Members of the League undertake to respect and preserve as against external aggression the territorial integrity and existing political independence of all Members of the League. In case of any such aggression or in case of any threat or danger of such

aggression the Council shall advise upon the means by which this obligation shall be fulfilled.

The structure erected was the League itself: an international parliament with an Assembly, in which all members were represented, and an executive Council, in which the great powers shared a larger responsibility with a minority of smaller states. In addition, there was a separate and independent judicial branch—a Permanent Court of International Justice, and an administrative arm—a Secretariat and various commissions charged with the responsibility to execute the peace treaties and to promote international cooperation in economic and social fields. It was, Wilson said when he first presented the Covenant to a full session of the conference, "a living thing . . . a definite guarantee of peace . . . against the things which have just come near bringing the whole structure of civilization into ruin."

Did Wilson fail at Paris? This is a question that has been asked and answered a thousand times by statesmen and scholars since the Versailles Treaty was signed in 1919. It will be asked so long as men remember Woodrow Wilson and the world's first major effort to prevent future aggressions and wars. The answer that one gives depends, not only upon the circumstances and mood prevailing at the time it is given, but also upon the view that one takes of history and of the potentialities and limitations of human endeavor. That is to say, it makes a great deal of difference whether one judges Wilson's work by absolute so-called moral standards, or whether one views what he did while remembering the obstacles that he faced, the pressures under which he labored, what was possible and what impossible to achieve at the time, and what would have happened had he not been present at the conference.

The Versailles Treaty, measured by the standards that Wilson had enunciated from 1916 to 1919, obviously failed to fulfill entirely the liberal peace program. It was not, as Wilson had demanded in his "Peace without Victory" speech and implicitly promised in the Fourteen Points Address, a peace among equals. It was, rather, as the Germans contended then and later, a *diktat* imposed by victors upon a beaten foe. It shouldered Germany with a reparations liability that was both economically difficult for Germany to satisfy and potentially a source of future international conflict.* It satisfied the victors' demands for a division of the enemy's colonies and territories. In several important instances, it violated the principle of self-determination. Finally, it was filled with pinpricks, like Article 231 and the provision for the trial of the former German Emperor, that served no purpose except to humiliate the German people. It does not, therefore, require much argument to prove that Wilson failed to win the settlement that he had demanded and that the Allies had promised in the Pre-Armistice Agreement.

To condemn Wilson because he failed in part is, however, to miss the entire moral of our story. That moral is a simple one: The Paris peace settlement reveals more clearly than any other episode of the twentieth century both the tension between the ideal and the real in history, and the truth of the proposition that failure inheres in all human striving. It does not make much sense merely to list Wilson's failures. We can see their meaning only when we understand *why* he failed to the extent that he did.

Wilson did not succeed wholly at Paris because he did not fight with all his mind and strength for the liberal peace program. Never before had he fought more tenaciously or pleaded more eloquently. Nor did he fail because he was incompetent, uninformed, and "bamboozled" by men of superior wit and learning, as John Maynard

*John Maynard Keynes, in his influential *Economic Consequences of the Peace* (1920), conclusively proved the utter economic absurdity of the reparations provisions to a whole postwar generation of scholars in England and America. It is no longer possible to be quite so dogmatic, for Étienne Mantoux, in *The Carthaginian Peace, or The Economic Consequences of Mr. Keynes* (1952), has proved that Keynes was wrong in his statistical methods and has demonstrated that German resources were in fact fully adequate to satisfy the reparations requirements of the Versailles Treaty. This position is supported by many economists and by the late Samuel Flagg Bemis in his *Diplomatic History of the United States* (1955). They point out that Hitler spent vastly more money on rearmament than the German nation would have paid in reparations during the 1930s.

These arguments, actually, are unanswerable, but in a larger sense they are also irrelevant. The question is, not whether it was possible for the Germans to continue reparations payments over a long period, but whether they were willing to do so; whether the British and French would attempt to coerce the Germans for a long period if the Germans were not willing to continue voluntary payments; and whether the monetary returns were worth all the international ill will that they provoked. To ask the question this way is, it seems to me, to answer it.

Keynes, in *The Economic Consequences of the Peace,* and Harold Nicolson, in *Peacemaking 1919* (1933), have portrayed him in their unkind caricatures. Indeed, the records of the deliberations at Paris demonstrate conclusively that Wilson was the best-informed and on the whole the wisest man among the statesmen assembled there.

Wilson failed as he did because his handicaps and the obstacles he fought against made failure inevitable. First and foremost, he had lost most of his strategic advantages by the time the peace conference opened. German military power, upon which he had relied as a balance against Allied ambitions, was now totally gone. Wilson had no lever to use against Britain and France, for they were no longer dependent upon American men and resources for survival. His only recourse—withdrawal from the conference—would have resulted in a Carthaginian peace imposed by the French, as the British alone could have prevented the French from carrying out their plans to destroy Germany. In these circumstances, compromise was not merely desirable; it was a compelling necessity to avert, from Wilson's point of view, a far worse alternative.

To compound Wilson's difficulties, his claim to the right to speak in the name of the American people, already seriously weakened by the election of a Republican Congress in November 1918, was denied during the peace conference itself by Republican leaders like Senator Henry Cabot Lodge. In addition, Colonel House, upon whom Wilson had relied as his strong right arm, had failed to support liberal peace ideals during that period of the conference when he was still the President's spokesman. Not only did House became a captive of Clemenceau, he was so eager for harmony that he seriously undercut and compromised Wilson on several crucial occasions.

The character of Wilson's antagonists at Paris also posed a formidable obstacle. Clemenceau, Lloyd George, Orlando, Baron Sonnino, and the Japanese delegates were all tough and resourceful negotiators, masters of the game of diplomacy, quick to seize every advantage that the less experienced American offered.

To overcome such opposition, Wilson had at his command the threat of withdrawal, the promise of American support for the right kind of settlement and of leadership in the League of Nations, and the fact that he did speak for liberal groups, not only in his own country, but throughout the world as well. These were sources of considerable strength, to be sure, but they were not enough to enable Wilson to *impose his own settlement.*

Finally, Wilson's desire for "open covenants, openly arrived at" was frustrated by the absolute refusal of his European colleagues at Paris to permit what Wilson urged—direct press observance of the conference's proceedings. However, Wilson on his own gave full, daily briefings to his liaison with the press, Ray Stannard Baker. Consequently, the Paris Peace Conference was the best-reported such conference in history to that time, and there were no secret treaties negotiated at Paris in 1919.*

In spite of it all, Wilson won a settlement that honored more of the fourteen points than it violated and which to a large degree vindicated his liberal ideals. Belgium was restored, Alsace-Lorraine was returned to France, and an independent Poland with access to the sea was created. The claims of the Central European and Balkan peoples to self-determination were satisfied. German military power was destroyed, at least for a time. Most important, the Paris settlement provided machinery for its own revision through the League of Nations and the hope that the passing of time and American leadership in the League would help to heal the world's wounds and build a future free from fear.**

As it turned out, many of Wilson's expectations were fulfilled even though the American people refused to play the part assigned to them. As intimated earlier, the reparations problem was finally solved in the 1920s and early 1930s in a way not dissimilar from the method that Wilson had proposed. Germany was admitted to the League in 1926, and that organization then ceased to be a mere league of victors. Substantial naval disarmament and limitation were accomplished in

---

*Wilson's phrase "open convenants, openly arrived at" is still strangely misunderstood. He did not mean to rule out confidential communication in diplomacy. What he really meant was that there should be no more secret treaties—the one thing that all international liberals agreed upon.

**It should be added that one of the fourteen points, the issue of the freedom of the seas, became moot once the Covenant of the League was adopted. As Wilson pointed out, there would be no neutrals and neutral rights in the event of a future war in violation of the guarantees embodied in the Covenant.

1921 and 1930. Even the great and hitherto elusive goal of land disarmament and the recognition of Germany's right to military equality were seriously sought by international action in the early 1930s. In brief, the Paris settlement, in spite of its imperfections, did create a new international order that functioned reasonably well, relatively speaking.

It is time to stop perpetuating the myth that the Paris settlement made inevitable the rise to power of Mussolini, the Japanese militarists, and Hitler, and hence the Second World War. That war was primarily the result of the Great Depression, which wrought great havoc particularly in Japan and Central Europe and devastated the international economy. In turn, the depression caused all nations to follow selfish policies and eschew international cooperation. The Second World War was also caused by the failure of the United States and Great Britain, in the midst of the depression, to stop Japanese aggression in Manchuria in 1931, and by the loss of British and French nerve in dealing with Hitler from 1935 to 1938. It was, additionally, caused by British fear of the Soviet Union and the delusion that Hitler might be used as a counterweight to the Soviets.

The Paris Peace Conference was for Wilson more a time of heroic striving and impressive achievement than of failure. Against odds that would have caused weaker men to surrender, he was able to prevent a Carthaginian kind of peace, and at the same time he created the machinery for the gradual attainment of the kind of settlement that he would have liked to impose at once. The Paris settlement, therefore, was not inevitably a "lost peace." On the contrary, it established the foundation of what could have been a viable and secure world order, if only the victors had maintained the will to build upon it.

5

Wilson and the Fight for the League of Nations

Wilson returned to the United States in June 1919 to face the crucial task of winning the support of the American people and the approval of the Senate for the Versailles Treaty, the underpinning of the Paris settlements. During the months following Wilson's homecoming, indeed until the election of 1920, there ensued in the United States a debate no less important than the great debate of 1787–1789 over ratification of the Constitution. At stake was the issue of American participation in a new world order capped by the League of Nations, an instrumentality designed to promote world cooperation and peace and armed with sanctions (including military force) to prevent aggression.

Some details of the well-known parliamentary struggle and of the bitter personal controversy between Wilson and his chief antagonist, Senator Henry Cabot Lodge of Massachusetts, cannot be ignored. However, the emphasis of this chapter will be upon what has often been obscured by too much focus on the dramatic details—how the great debate of 1919–1920 revealed differences in opinion concerning the role that the United States should play in world affairs. These differences were fundamental and authentic because they transcended partisanship and personality. They also are as relevant to Americans in the latter part of this century as they were in Wilson's day.

The general lines of battle over ratification of the Treaty of Versailles were drawn before Wilson went to Paris, and largely by Wilson himself. Wilson's appeal during the congressional campaign had given a partisan coloration to the whole process of peacemaking. Many Republicans had regarded Wilson's appointment to the American Peace Commission of only one nominal Republican—Henry White, a career diplomat—as a slap in the face. By ignoring the Senate in his appointment of the commission, moreover, Wilson made it inevitably certain that the fight over the Treaty would renew in virulent form the old conflict between the President and the upper house for control of foreign policy.*

It would be a great mistake to assume, as some historians have done, that the fate of the Treaty was foreordained by the injection of partisanship into the question of peacemaking or by Wilson's failure to appoint senators to the commission. In the subsequent controversy, Wilson had the warm support of the League to Enforce Peace, composed mainly of prominent Republicans, including former President William Howard Taft. The debate in the country over the Treaty was not a partisan one; and, in the final analysis, the votes in the Senate were partisan only to the degree that a large number of Democratic senators followed Wilson's demands. The important point is that the country at large and the Senate, to a large degree, divided over profoundly important issues, not along party lines. Finally, the fact that Wilson took no senators with him to Paris was of no consequence for the final result.

While Wilson was in Paris, there were unmistakable signs at

*Wilson did consider appointing senators to the American Peace Commission. The problem was that, if he had appointed the ranking Democratic member of the Foreign Relations Committee, he would also have had to appoint the ranking Republican, Lodge. Wilson and Lodge were barely on speaking terms at this time. Worse still, Lodge was perhaps the preeminent spokesman in the United States for the old diplomacy. He wanted a vengeful and punitive peace. He had said publicly and in letters to highly placed friends in England and France that Wilson did not speak for the American people. Wilson knew that there was no way that he could work with Lodge in Paris; indeed, Lodge's appointment might have created havoc there. Thus Wilson's decision not to appoint any senators seems inevitable.

There remains the question why Wilson did not appoint other prominent Republicans like former President William Howard Taft, Elihu Root, or Charles Evans Hughes. He would not appoint Root because he thought that he was a reactionary and a symbol of the "old" diplomacy. Wilson probably did not appoint Taft or Hughes because he knew that if either one or both accompanied him to Paris, he would have to give them a share in decision making, and he did not relish the thought of having to make compromises with them as well as with the Allied leaders.

home that he would encounter significant opposition in the Senate. The most ominous of these was the so-called Round Robin resolution that Lodge read to the Senate on March 4, 1919. It was signed by thirty-seven senators, more than enough to defeat the Treaty, and declared that the Covenant of the League of Nations, "in the form now proposed to the peace conference," was unacceptable. At the same time, isolationists in the Senate were already beginning a furious rhetorical attack against the Covenant.

Although Wilson was defiant in a speech in New York just before he sailed for Paris, he did accept the advice of his friends who urged him to conciliate his critics. He first tried, through Henry White, to ascertain precisely why the Covenant was not acceptable to Lodge and the signers of the Round Robin. Then, when Lodge refused to give any specifics, Wilson consulted Taft and other Republican supporters of the League and, in response to their suggestions, obtained changes in the Covenant. They provided for the right of member nations of the League to withdraw after giving due notice, exempted domestic questions from the League's jurisdiction, permitted member nations to refuse to accept a colonial mandate, and, most important, accorded formal recognition to the Monroe Doctrine.

Wilson was exhausted by the end of the peace conference and showed numerous indications of an unwillingness to compromise further with his senatorial critics. Colonel House, on the day that Wilson left Paris, urged him to meet the Senate in a conciliatory spirit. "I have found," Wilson is alleged to have replied, "that one can never get anything in this life that is worthwhile without fighting for it." This self-referential statement suggests that Wilson felt a great burden of guilt because of the compromises that he had made. If this was true, then the guilt feelings were reinforcing his determination to make no further compromises.

Refreshed by the return voyage, Wilson returned to Washington on July 8 in a confident mood. And with good reason. Much of the senatorial criticism of the Treaty was captious. Most important, by this time thirty-two state legislatures had endorsed the Covenant in concurrent resolutions; thirty-three governors had expressed their approval; and a *Literary Digest* poll indicated overwhelming support for the Covenant among editors of newspapers and magazines. Indeed, the whole country seemed to be in a fever of excitement about the League.

Wilson was, therefore, in the mood of a triumphant leader presenting his adversaries with a *fait accompli* when he laid the Treaty formally before the Senate on July 10. He did not refer to the senators, as he had often done, as his "colleagues," and he did not use his favorite phrase "common counsel," that is, the necessity of reasonable give and take before arriving at a final decision. On the contrary, he "informed" the senators that a world settlement had been made and then took the highest possible ground to urge prompt and unqualified approval. The League of Nations, he exclaimed, was the best hope of mankind. "Dare we reject it and break the heart of the world?" He gave the answer in an impromptu peroration at the end:

> The stage is set, the destiny disclosed. It has come about by no plan of our conceiving, but by the hand of God who led us into this way. We cannot turn back. We can only go forward, with lifted eyes and freshened spirit, to follow the vision. It was of this that we dreamed at our birth. America shall in truth show the way. The light streams upon the path ahead, and nowhere else.

Wilson met reporters in an informal press conference after delivering this address. He was relaxed and confident. There had been much talk of reservations to the Treaty. What did the President think of that idea? Wilson replied that he was determined to oppose all reservations, for they would require a two-thirds vote of the Senate and necessitate renegotiation of the Treaty. It is significant that a constitutional scholar should have made such a mistake. He had no doubt that the Treaty would be ratified just as it stood.*

---

*I have been unable to find the source of the account given in Thomas A. Bailey, *Woodrow Wilson and the Great Betrayal* (1945), p. 9. According to this account, a reporter asked Wilson if the Treaty could be ratified with reservations. Wilson shot back: "I do not think hypothetical questions are concerned. *The Senate is going to ratify the treaty.*" Another story that Bailey relates (*ibid.,* pp. 14–15) seems to be anachronistic. Bailey says that the French Ambassador, Jusserand, went to see Wilson to urge him to consent to ratification with reservations. To the Ambassador's horror, Wilson replied: "Mr. Ambassador, I shall consent to nothing. *The Senate must take its medicine.*"

Actually, the situation was far less simple and reassuring than Wilson imagined at the beginning of the great debate. For one thing, powerful voices were already raised in outright and violent condemnation of the Treaty on various grounds. Idealists, who had thrilled at Wilson's vision of a new world, condemned the Treaty because it failed to establish a millennial order. The German-Americans believed that the Treaty was a base betrayal of the Fatherland; the Italian-Americans were angry over Wilson's opposition to Italy's demands. Most important, the several million Irish-Americans, inflamed by the civil war then raging in Ireland, were up in arms because Wilson had refused to win Irish independence at Paris and because the Treaty allegedly benefited the hated English. The powerful chain of Hearst newspapers was marshaling and inciting all the hyphenate protests. Out-and-out isolationists believed that American membership in the League of Nations would mean entanglement in all of Europe's rivalries and wars. They had powerful advocates in a small group of so-called irreconcilables or bitter-enders in the Senate, led by Hiram W. Johnson of California, William E. Borah of Idaho, and James A. Reed of Missouri, who opposed the Treaty for various deeply rooted reasons—nationalism, chauvinism, and idealism.

These were the major groups who opposed ratification of the Treaty. In the ensuing debate, they were the loudest and busiest participants of all. They were, however, a minority among the leaders of thought and political opinion, and they spoke for a minority of the people, at least before 1920, if not afterward. This is a simple point but a vital one, because, in its important aspects, the debate over the Treaty was not a struggle between advocates of complete withdrawal on the one side and proponents of total international commitment on the other. It was, rather, a contest between the champions of a potentially strong system of collective security and a group who favored a more limited commitment. It was a choice between these alternatives, and not between complete isolation or complete internationalism, that Wilson, the Senate, and the American people eventually had to make. We will, therefore, let the arguments of the isolationists pass without analysis and concentrate our attention upon the two main and decisive courses of the debate.

Differences of opinion in the United States over the territorial and other provisions of the Treaty were insignificant as compared to the differences evoked by the Covenant of the League and its provisions to prevent aggression and war. Those provisions were clear and for the most part unequivocal. Article 10 guaranteed the political independence and territorial integrity of every member nation throughout the world. Articles 11, 12, 13, 15, 16, and 17 established the machinery of arbitration for all international disputes susceptible to that procedure and decreed that an act of war against one member nation should *"ipso facto* be deemed to . . . [be] an act of war against all the other Members" and should be followed automatically by an economic blockade against the aggressor and by Council action to determine what military measures should be used to repel the aggression. These were almost ironclad guarantees of mutual security, meant to be effective and unencumbered by the right of any nation involved in a dispute to veto action by the League's Council. Whether such a worldwide system could work, and whether the American people were prepared at this stage of their development to support such a system even if it did work—these were the two main issues of the great debate of 1919–1920.

The decisive opposition to the Versailles Treaty came from a group of men who, to a varying degree, would have answered no to both these questions. This group included some of the most distinguished leaders in and out of the Senate, like Senator Frank B. Kellogg of Minnesota, President Nicholas Murray Butler of Columbia University, former Secretary of State Elihu Root, and Charles Evans Hughes, Republican presidential candidate in 1916. Most of them were Republicans, because few Democrats active in politics dared to incur the President's wrath by opposing him. They were not isolationists but limited internationalists who believed that the United States should play, in a varying degree, an active role in preserving the peace of the world. Most of them favored, for example, arbitration, the establishment of something like a World Court to interpret and codify international law, and international agreements for disarmament, economic cooperation, and the like. Some of them even supported the idea of alliances with certain powers for specific purposes.

On the other hand, all the limited internationalists opposed any such approval of the Treaty as would commit the United States

unreservedly to the kind of collective security the Covenant of the
League had created. Their arguments might be summarized as follows:

First, a system of collective security that is worldwide in opera-
tion is not likely either to work or to endure the strains that will
inevitably be put upon it, because in practice the great powers will not
accept the limitations that the Covenant places upon their sovereignty, and no nation will go to war to vindicate Article 10 unless its
vital interests compel it to do so. Such sweeping guarantees as the
Covenant affords are, therefore, worse than no guarantees at all because they offer only an illusory hope of security.

Second, the Covenant's fundamental guarantee, embodied in Article 10, is impossible to maintain because its promise to perpetuate
the *status quo* defies the very law of life. As Elihu Root put it:

> If perpetual, it would be an attempt to preserve for all time
> unchanged the distribution of power and territory made in ac-
> cordance with the views and exigencies of the Allies in this
> present juncture of affairs. It would necessarily be futile. . . . It
> would not only be futile; it would be mischievious. Change and
> growth are the law of life, and no generation can impose its will
> in regard to the growth of nations and the distribution of power
> upon succeeding generations.

Third, the American people are not ready to support the Covenant's sweeping commitments and in fact should not do so unless their
vital interests are involved in a dispute. They would and should be
ready to act to prevent the outbreak or any conflict that threatened
to lead to a general war, but it is inconceivable that they would or
should assume the risk of war to prevent a border dispute in the
Balkans, or to help maintain Japanese control of Shantung Province
or British supremacy in Ireland and India. Unconditional ratification
of the Treaty by the United States would, therefore, be worse than
outright rejection, for it would mean the making of promises that the
American people could not possibly honor in the future.

Fourth, unqualified membership in the League will raise grave
dangers to American interests and the American constitutional sys-

tem. It will menace American control over immigration and tariff policies, imperil the Monroe Doctrine, increase the power of the President at the expense of Congress, and necessitate the maintenance of a large standing army for the fulfillment of obligations under the Covenant.

Fifth, and most important, full-fledged participation in such a system of collective security as the Covenant establishes will spell the end of American security in foreign affairs, because it will mean transferring the power of decision over questions of peace and war from the President and Congress to an international agency which the United States could not control.

The limited internationalists, voicing these objections day in and day out as the great debate reached its crescendo in the autumn of 1919, made their purposes and program indelibly clear. They would accept most of the provisions of the Treaty unrelated to the League and acquiesce in the ones that they did not like. They would also sanction American membership in the League of Nations. But they would also insist upon reserving to the United States, and specifically to Congress, the power of decision concerning the degree of American participation in the League; and they would make no binding promise to enforce collective security anywhere in the future. This strategy was devised by Elihu Root in July 1919.

This was also the final, public position of Senator Lodge, the man who devised and executed the Republican strategy in the upper house during the parliamentary phase of the Treaty struggle. Personally, Lodge had little hope for the success of the League, a profound contempt for Wilson, and almost a sardonic scorn for Wilson's international ideals. The Massachusetts Senator was an ardent nationalist, almost a jingoist. He was no isolationist, but a believer in a strong balance of power. His solution would have been harsh terms, including dismemberment of Germany, and the formation of an Anglo-Franco-American alliance as the best insurance for future peace. But, as chairman of the Foreign Relations Committee and leader of his party in the Senate, it was his duty to subordinate his own strong feelings and to find a common ground upon which most Republicans could stand. That common ground, that program acceptable to an overwhelming majority of Republicans inside the Senate and out, was, in brief, to approve the Treaty and to accept membership in the League. This would be subject to certain amendments and reservations that would achieve the objectives of the limited internationalists.

Amendments and reservations designed to statisfy the moderate internationalists were embodied in the report that the Republican majority of the Foreign Relations Committee presented to the Senate on September 10, 1919. During the following weeks, that body rejected the amendments (on the ground that they would require renegotiation of the Treaty) and adopted most of them in the form of reservations, fourteen in all. Most of them were unimportant, but there was one that constituted a virtual rejection of the kind of collective security that Wilson had envisaged. It was Reservation 2, which declared that the United States assumed no obligations to preserve the territorial integrity or political independence of any other country, unless Congress should by act or joint resolution specifically assume such an obligation. In addition, the preamble to the reservations provided that American ratification of the Treaty should not take effect until at least three of the four principal Allied powers had accepted the reservations in a formal exchange of notes.

This, then, was the program to which most of Wilson's opponents stood committed by the time that the Senate moved toward a formal vote on the Versailles Treaty. Whether Lodge himself was an irreconcilable who desired the defeat of the Treaty, or whether he was merely a strong reservationist, is an important question but an irrelevant one at this point. The significant fact is that he had succeeded in uniting most Republicans and in committing them to a program that affirmed limited internationalism at the same time that it repudiated American support of a tentative collective security system.

Meanwhile, despite his earlier show of intransigence, Wilson had been hard at work in preparation for the impending struggle. In an effort to split the Republican ranks, he held a series of conferences in late July with eleven Republican senators who he thought would favor approval of the Treaty after the adoption of a few interpretive reservations. On August 19, the President met the Foreign Relations Committee at the White House for a three-hour grilling on all phases of the settlement. The interchange produced no new support for the

Treaty. What Wilson did not know, and never did seem to know, was that virtually all of the so-called mild reservationists had already coalesced into the central hard-core Republican pro-League group in the Senate. They were the men who voted with Democrats to convert Lodge's amendments into reservations. They were the ones who forced Lodge, for the sake of party unity, to support the treaty with reservations. Finally, they were the real authors of the reservations. Thus, confer as much as he could, Wilson made no headway in winning the support that would be vital when the Senate voted on the Treaty.

In response, Wilson made one of the most fateful decisions of his career. It was, as he put it, to go to the people and purify the wells of public opinion that had been poisoned by the isolationists and opponents of unreserved ratification. He was physically weakened by his labors at Paris, and his physician warned that a long speaking tour might endanger his life. Even so, he insisted upon making the effort to rally the people, the sources of authority, who had always sustained him in the past.

Wilson left Washington on September 3, 1919, and headed for the heartland of America, into Ohio, Indiana, Missouri, Iowa, Nebraska, Minnesota, and the Dakotas—into the region where isolationist sentiment was strongest. From there he campaigned through the Northwest and the major cities of the Pacific Coast. The final leg of his journey took him through Nevada, Utah, Wyoming, and Colorado, where the tour ended after Wilson's partial breakdown on September 25 and 26. In all he traveled 8,000 miles in twenty-two days and delivered thirty-two major addresses and eight minor ones. It was not only the greatest single speaking effort of Wilson's career, but also one of the most notable forensic accomplishments in American history.

Everywhere that he went, Wilson pleaded in good temper, not as a partisan, but as a leader who stood above party strife and advantage. He was making his tour, he explained, first of all so that the people might know the truth about the Treaty of Versailles and no longer be confused by the misrepresentations of its enemies. As he put it at Oakland and at Reno:

One thing has been impressed upon me more than another as I have crossed the continent, and that is that the people of the United States have been singularly and, I some time fear deliberately, misled as to the character and contents of the treaty of peace.

Some of the critics . . . are looking backward. . . . Their power to divert, or to pervert, the view of this whole thing has made it necessary for me repeatedly on this journey to take the liberty that I am going to take with you tonight—of telling you just what kind of a treaty this is.

In almost every speech, therefore, Wilson explicitly described and defended the major provisions of the Treaty and the purposes of its framers. He defended the severity of the articles relating to Germany, on the ground that her crimes against civilization demanded stern punishment. He answered the critics of the Shantung settlement, first by frankly admitting that he did not like the provisions for Japanese control and, next, by declaring that he had obtained the only possible settlement that offered any hope for China's eventual recovery of the province. In a similar manner he tried to answer other criticisms, and he concluded, not by denying that there were imperfections in the Treaty, but by declaring that they were more than counterbalanced by the constructive achievements.

Wilson's supreme purpose was, of course, not to explain the controverted provisions of the Treaty relating to territories, colonies, and reparations, but rather to defend the League of Nations against its traducers, to explain the Covenant's system of collective security, and to call the American people to the world leadership that he said history now demanded of them.

He began usually by saying that the League of Nations was the fulfillment of an old American dream of peace, that it was an attempt to apply the principles of the Monroe Doctrine to the world at large, that the suggestion of such an organization had come in recent times as much if not more from Republicans than from Democrats, and that he had simply translated American ideas and proposals into statutory form and insisted that they be embodied in the Treaty.

Wilson then proceeded to describe the provisions of the Cove-

114

nant, to show how they would work in actual practice, and to attempt to prove that they afforded a system *for maintaining peace instead of for waging war.* Article 10, he was fond of emphasizing, was the heart of the Covenant and the foundation of the new world order. "Article 10," he said at Indianapolis, "speaks the conscience of the world." "Article 10," he added at Reno,

> is the heart of the enterprise. Article 10 is the test of the honor and courage and endurance of the world. Article 10 says that every member of the League, and that means every fighting power in the world, . . . solemnly engages to respect and preserve as against external aggression the territorial integrity and existing political independence of the other members of the League. If you do that, you have absolutely stopped ambitious and aggressive war . . . [for] as against external aggression, as against ambition, as against the desire to dominate from without, we all stand together in a common pledge, and that pledge is essential to the peace of the world.

In answer to the charge that unconditional affirmation of Article 10 would involve the United States perpetually in war, Wilson replied by saying that the League was primarily an instrument of peace. Future wars would be virtually impossible if the provisions of the Covenant implementing Article 10 were observed and enforced by the members of the League. Primarily, nations engaged in a dispute that might lead to war were bound to submit their controversy either to arbitration, the World Court, or the Council of the League. Should any nation go to war in violation of these promises, then all the other members of the League would automatically institute a total blockade, "financial, commercial, and personal," against the aggressor.

As Wilson explained at Kansas City:

> We absolutely boycott them [the aggressors]. . . . There shall be no communication even between them and the rest of the world. They shall receive no goods; they shall ship no goods. They shall receive no telegraphic messages; they shall send none. They shall receive no mail; no mail will be received from them. The nationals, the citizens, of the member states will never enter their territory until the matter is adjusted, and their citizens cannot

115

leave their territory. It is the most complete boycott ever conceived in a public document, and I want to say to you with confident prediction that there will be no more fighting after that.

It was conceivable, of course, Wilson admitted, that war would occur in spite of all these precautions. "Nobody in his senses claims for the Covenant . . . that it is certain to stop war," he said at Indianapolis. If an aggressor flouted the provisions of the Covenant, and if economic measures did not suffice to stop the aggression, then war would probably occur. If it was a major conflagration, then the United States could not remain neutral in any event. If it was a minor controversy far removed from the Western Hemisphere, then the United States would not be directly involved. Enemies of the League had charged that membership in that body would mean American involvement in every dispute everywhere in the world. "If you want to put out a fire in Utah," the President replied at Salt Lake City,

you do not send to Oklahoma for the fire engine. If you want to put out a fire in the Balkans, if you want to stamp out the smoldering flame in some part of central Europe, you do not send to the United States for troops. The Council of the League selects the powers which are most ready, most available, most suitable, and selects them only at their own consent, so that the United States would in no such circumstances conceivably be drawn in unless the flame spread to the world.

Isolationists were charging that membership in the League would impair American sovereignty and require the fulfillment of unpleasant duties. Wilson replied that the contention was, of course, true in part. In Billings, Montana, he said: "The only way in which you can have impartial determinations in this world is by consenting to something you do not want to do. . . . Every time you have a case in court, one or the other of the parties has to consent to do something he does not want to do. . . . Yet we regard that as the foundation of civilization, that we will not fight about these things, and that when we lose in court we will take our medicine."

It seemed almost superfluous, Wilson added, to argue the necessity of American membership in the League of Nations. There was the obvious fact, he declared at Des Moines, that American isolation had ended, "not because we chose to go into the politics of the world, but because by the sheer genius of this people and the growth of our power we have become a determining factor in the history of mankind, and after you have become a determining factor you cannot remain isolated, whether you want to or not." The only question confronting the American people was, therefore, whether they would exercise their influence in the world, which could henceforth be profound and controlling, in partnership with the other powers or in defiance of them. Standing alone, he warned, meant defying the world; defying the world meant maintaining a great standing army and navy; and such militarism and navalism meant the end of democracy at home.

There was the additional fact that, without American participation and leadership, the League of Nations would become merely another armed alliance instead of a true concert of power. "It would be an alliance," Wilson declared at St. Louis,

> in which the partnership would be between the more powerful European nations and Japan, and the . . . antagonist, the disassociated party, the party standing off to be watched by the alliance, would be the United States of America. There can be no league of nations in the true sense without the partnership of this great people.

Without American participation and leadership, therefore, the League would fail. Without the League, there could be no hope for an effective collective security system. Without collective security, wars would come again. American participation was, therefore, essential to peace—the most vital and elemental interest of the United States. This became increasingly the main theme of Wilson's addresses as he journeyed deeper into the West. Over and over he cried out warnings like these:

> Ah, my fellow citizens, do not forget the aching hearts that are behind discussions like this. Do not forget the forlorn homes

117

from which those boys went and to which they never came back. I have it in my heart that if we do not do this great thing now, every woman ought to weep because of the child in her arms. If she has a boy at her breast, she may be sure that when he comes to manhood this terrible task will have to be done once more. Everywhere we go, the train, when it stops, is surrounded with little children, and I look at them almost with tears in my eyes, because I feel my mission is to save them. These glad youngsters with flags in their hands—I pray God that they may never have to carry that flag upon the battlefield!

Why, my fellow citizens, nothing brings a lump into my throat quicker on this journey I am taking than to see the thronging children that are everywhere the first, just out of childish curiosity and glee, no doubt, to crowd up to the train when it stops, because I know that, if by any chance, we should not win this great fight for the League of Nations, it would be their death warrant. They belong to the generation which would then have to fight the final war, and in that final war there would not be merely seven and a half million men slain. The very existence of civilization would be in the balance. . . . Stop for a moment to think about the next war, if there should be one. I do not hesitate to say that the war we have just been through, though it was shot through with terror of every kind, is not to be compared with the war we would have to face next time. . . . Ask any soldier if he wants to go through a hell like that again. The soldiers know what the next war would be. They know what the inventions were that were just about to be used for the absolute destruction of mankind. I am for any kind of insurance against a barbaric reversal of civilization.

Who were the enemies of the League and of the future peace of the world? They were, Wilson declared, the outright isolationists and the men who would destroy the charter of mankind by crippling reservations. They were little Americans, provincials, men of narrow vision. "They are ready to go back to that old and ugly plan of armed nations, of alliances, of watchful jealousies, of rabid antagonisms, of purposes concealed, running by the subtle channels of intrigue through the veins of people who do not dream what poison is being injected into their systems." "When at last in the annals of mankind they are gibbeted, they will regret that the gibbet is so high."

One by one, Wilson answered the specific criticisms of the Covenant relating to the Monroe Doctrine, the right of members to withdraw, and the question whether the League had any jurisdiction over the domestic affairs of members nations. He told how he had obtained revisions of the Covenant to satisfy American doubts about its first draft. These amendments, he continued, were embodied in the Covenant and were written in language as explicit as he knew how to devise. He would not object to reservations that merely clarified the American understanding of these questions. Reservations that in any way changed the meaning of the Covenant were, however, more serious, because they would require the renegotiation of the Treaty.

There remained the greatest threat of all to the integrity of the Covenant, the challenge of the reservation to Article 10. This reservation, Wilson warned, would destroy the foundation of any collective security, because it was a notice to the world that the American people would fulfill their obligations only when it suited their purposes to do so. "That," the President exclaimed at Salt Lake City, "is a rejection of the Covenant. That is an absolute refusal to carry any part of the same responsibility that the other members of the League carry." "In other words, my fellow citizens," he added at Cheyenne,

what this proposes is this: That we should make no general promise, but leave the nations associated with us to guess in each instance what we were going to consider ourselves bound to do and what we were not going to consider ourselves bound to do. It is as if you said, "We will not join the League definitely, but we will join it occasionally. We will not promise anything, but from time to time we may cooperate. We will not assume any obligations. . . ." This reservation proposes that we should not acknowledge any moral obligation in the matter; that we should stand off and say, "We will see, from time to time; consult us when you get into trouble, and then we will have a debate, and after two or three months we will tell you what we are going to do." The thing is unworthy and ridiculous, and I want to say distinctly that, as I read this, it would change the entire meaning of the Treaty and exempt the United States from all responsibil-

119

ity for the preservation of peace. It means the rejection of the Treaty, my fellow countrymen, nothing less. It means that the United States would take from under the structure its very foundations and support.

The irony of it all was, Wilson added, that the reservation was actually unnecessary, *if the objective of its framers was merely to reserve the final decision for war to the American government.* In the case of all disputes to which it was not a party, the United States would have an actual veto over the Council's decision for war, because that body could not advise member nations to go to war except by unanimous vote, exclusive of the parties to the dispute. Thus, Wilson explained, there was absolutely no chance that the United States could be forced into war against its will, unless it was itself guilty of aggression, in which case it would be at war anyway.

These were, Wilson admitted, legal technicalities, and, he added, he would not base his case for American participation in the League of Nations upon them. The issue was not who had the power to make decisions for war, but whether the American people were prepared to go wholeheartedly into the League, were determined to support a collective security system unreservedly, and were willing to make the sacrifices that were necessary to preserve peace. Wilson summarized all his pleading with unrivaled feeling at the Mormon capital:

> Instead of wishing to ask to stand aside, get the benefits of the League, but share none of its burdens or responsibilities, I for my part want to go in and accept what is offered to us, the leadership of the world. A leadership of what sort, my fellow citizens? Not a leadership that leads men along the lines by which great nations can profit out of weak nations. Not an exploiting power, but a liberating power—a power to show the world that when America was born it was indeed a finger pointed toward those lands into which men could deploy some of these days and live in happy freedom, look each other in the eyes as equals, see that no man was put upon, that no people were forced to accept authority which was not of their own choice, and that, out of the general generous impulse of the human genius and the human spirit, we were lifted along the levels of civilization to days when

there should be wars no more, but men should govern themselves in peace and amity and quiet. That is the leadership we said we wanted, and now the world offers it to us. It is inconceivable that we should reject it.

We come now to the well-known tragic sequel. Following his address at Pueblo, Colorado, on September 25, 1919, Wilson showed such obvious signs of exhaustion that his physician canceled his remaining engagements and sped the presidential train to Washington. On October 2, Wilson suffered a severe stroke and paralysis of the left side of his face and body. For several days his life hung in the balance; then he gradually revived, and by the end of October he was clearly out of danger. But his recovery was only partial at best. His mind remained relatively clear; but he was physically enfeebled, and the disease had wrecked his emotional constitution and aggravated all his more unfortunate personal traits.

Meanwhile, the Senate was nearing the end of its long debate over the Treaty of Versailles. Senator Lodge presented his revised fourteen reservations on behalf of the Foreign Relations Committee to the upper house on November 6, 1919. Senator Gilbert M. Hitchcock of Nebraska, the Democratic minority leader, countered with five reservations, four of which Wilson had approved in substance before he embarked upon his western tour. They simply sought to make clear the American understanding of Article 10 and other provisions of the Treaty. The issue before the Senate, therefore, now seemed clear—whether to approve the Treaty with reservations that did not impair the American obligation to uphold the Covenant, or whether to approve the Treaty with reservations that permitted repudiation of all compelling obligations and promised American support for only a limited international system.

Lodge beat down the Hitchcock reservations with the help of the irreconcilables and then won adoption of his own. Now Wilson had to choose between acceptance of the Lodge reservations or run the risk of the outright defeat of the Treaty. He gave his decision to Hitchcock in a brief conference at the White House on November 17 and in a letter on the following day: Under no circumstances could he accept the Lodge reservation to Article 10, for it meant nullification of the Treaty. When the Senate voted on November 19, therefore, most of the Democrats joined the irreconcilables to defeat approval with the Lodge reservations by a count of thirty-nine ayes to fifty-five nays. The Democratic leaders, hoping to split the Republican ranks and win the support of the mythical mild reservationists then moved unconditional approval of the Treaty. This strategy, upon which Wilson had placed all his hopes, failed, as a firm Republican majority defeated the resolution with the help of the irreconcilables by a vote of thirty-eight ayes to fifty-three nays.

The great mystery is why Wilson rejected the Lodge reservation to Article 10. Before he left on his western tour, Wilson handed Hitchcock four "interpretive" reservations to the articles relating to the right of member nations to withdraw, Article 10, the nonjurisdiction of the League over domestic matters like immigration, and the Monroe Doctrine. Wilson's reservation to Article 10 said that the Senate understood that the advice of the League Council with regard to the use of armed force was to be "regarded only as advice and leaves each member free to exercise its own judgment as to whether it [were] wise or practicable to act upon that advice or not." Hitchcock's own reservation, which presumably Wilson had approved, went even further and said that Congress would have to approve the use of armed force if so requested by the Council.

Why, when the two sides were so close together, did Wilson reject the Lodge reservation to Article 10? Having built so grandly at Paris, having fought so magnificently at home for his creation, why did he remove by his own hand the cornerstone of his edifice of peace? Were there inner demons of pride and arrogance driving him to what Thomas A. Bailey has called "the supreme infanticide"?

Dr. Weinstein has described the effects of the devastating stroke on Wilson's personality and perceptions at this time. He is convinced that, had Wilson been in full health, he would have found the formula to reconcile the differences between the Lodge and Hitchcock reservations. There is a great deal of evidence to support this hypothesis. When Wilson made his decision, on November 17, to reject the Lodge reservation, he was still a very sick man. His mind could function well in certain circumstances, but his whole emotional balance had been shattered. He was sick, petulant, and rigid. He saw very few people between his stroke and November 17, and those who talked to him were careful not to upset him. From his lonely isolation in a sickroom, he saw the outside world from a limited and distorted view. A healthy Wilson certainly would have spent most of his time from his return to Washington from the West to mid-November conferring, cajoling, and doing everything possible to find an acceptable compromise on the reservation to Article 10. This was part of the genius of his leadership. He had displayed it many times before, most notably in negotiating the writing of the Federal Reserve Act and the Versailles Treaty.

Wilson's isolation and the unfortunate pathological effects of his stroke might well have caused him to give the most literal reading possible to the Lodge reservation to Article 10. Taken literally, this reservation could be read as an emphatic repudiation of American responsibilities under the Covenant. It read:

> The United States assumes no obligation to preserve the territorial integrity or political independence of any other country or to interfere in controversies between nations—whether members of the league or not—under the provisions of Article 10, or to employ the military or naval forces of the United States under any article of the treaty for any purpose, unless in any particular case the Congress, which, under the Constitution, has the sole power to declare war or authorize the employment of the military or naval forces of the United States, shall by act or joint resolution so provide.

Even a healthy Wilson might have concluded that this reservation amounted, as he put it, to nullification of the Treaty. And any strong President would have bridled at the closing phrases of the reservation, for they constituted the first important congressional constraints against the President as commander in chief to this point in American history and were probably unconstitutional.

Wilson, whether because of his illness or not, did read the reservation literally. He believed, very deeply, that the one issue now at stake was whether the United States would join the League of Nations and give leadership to it wholeheartedly and without reservations, or whether it would join the League grudgingly, with no promises to help maintain the peace of the world. To Wilson, the difference between what he stood for and what the Republicans would agree to was the difference between the success or failure and the life or death of mankind's best hope for peace.

The vote on November 19 was not the end of the struggle, for during the following months an overwhelming majority of the leaders of opinion in the United States refused to accept the vote as the final verdict. In the absence of any reliable indices, it is impossible to measure the division of public opinion as a whole; but there can be little doubt that an overwhelming majority of thoughtful people favored ratification with some kind of reservations, even with the Lodge reservations, if that was necessary to obtain the Senate's consent.

Consequently, there was, enormous pressure upon the leaders in both parties for compromise during the last weeks of 1919 and the early months of 1920. Prominent Republicans who had taken leadership in a nonpartisan campaign for the League (including former President Taft), scores of editors, the spokesmen of various academic, religious, and labor organizations, and Democratic leaders who dared oppose the President (like William J. Bryan and Colonel House) begged Lodge and Wilson to find a common ground. Alarmed by the possibility of American rejection of the Treaty, spokesmen for the British government declared publicly that limited American participation in the League would be better than no participation at all.

Under this pressure, the moderate leaders in both camps set to work in late December and early January to find a basis for agreement. Even Lodge began to weaken and joined the bipartisan conferees who were attempting to work out an acceptable reservation to Article 10. But the Massachusetts Senator and his friends would not yield the essence of their reservation, and it was Wilson who had to make the final choice.

By January, Wilson had recovered sufficient strength to take personal leadership of the Democrats in the Senate. One effect of his stroke was a strong if not complete tendency to deny that he was ill. For example, he would refer to his paralyzed left arm as "it" and not as a part of his body. He was absolutely convinced that he had the great mass of the people behind him and that they would crush any senator or party who opposed him. Living as he did in a world of unreality, Wilson concocted two stratagems.

The first stratagem was to challenge the fifty-seven senators from thirty-eight states who opposed the Treaty altogether or supported the Lodge reservations to resign and then run for reelection in special elections. Should they be reelected, Wilson would appoint a leader of the opposition as Secretary of State and he, Wilson, and his Vice President would resign and the Republican leader would become President. This plan proved to be unfeasible because of variations in state election laws.*

Then Wilson, ever innovative, turned to his second stratagem—to make the treaty the leading issue of the coming presidential campaign. Moreover, he would be the Democratic nominee; he would go once again to the people and win an overwhelming mandate for the League. He even drafted a Democratic platform and his speech of acceptance. He set this plan in motion in a letter to the Jackson Day Dinner in Washington, then the chief meeting of Democrats preliminary to a presidential campaign, on January 8, 1920. He repeated his principal arguments for ungrudging approval, declared that "the overwhelming majority" of the people desired ratification of the Treaty, and concluded:

> If there is any doubt as to what the people of the country think on this vital matter, the clear and single way out is to submit it for determination at the next election to the voters of the nation, to give the next election the form of a great and solemn referendum, a referendum as to the part the United States is to play in completing the settlements of the war and in the prevention in the future of such outrages as Germany attempted to perpetrate.

The Jackson Day letter spelled disaster for ratification of the Treaty in any form. Wilson committed the supreme error of converting what had really not been a partisan issue, except in the parliamen-

---

*For example, senators in special elections were elected in some states by popular vote; in others, they were appointed by the governor until special popular elections could be held. There were other difficulties, too.

tary sense, into a hostage of party loyalty and politics. Henceforth most Republican senators would have to vote as Republicans, most Democrats as Democrats, even though they might want to put the interests of the country above those of party and vote for ratification with reservations.

Secondly, in spite of his unshakable faith in the wisdom of the people, Wilson, an expert in the American constitutional and political systems, should have known that there is no way to convert a presidential election into a referendum upon a single issue. Bryan had tried to make the election of 1900 a referendum upon the question of imperialism and had failed utterly to do so. As it turned out in 1920, Warren G. Harding, the Republican nominee and a strong reservationist, had no trouble in muting and sidestepping the League issue. Indeed, a group of thirty-one prominent pro-League Republicans issued a statement during the campaign assuring their fellow Republicans that Harding's election would be the best assurance of ratification and American membership in the League of Nations!

Thirdly, and ironically, Wilson's Jackson Day letter destroyed Wilson's leadership among the various segments of elite opinion makers who had heretofore been his strongest supporters—religious leaders, educational leaders, publicists, editors, and politically active professionals. A reading of their correspondence, journals, editorials, and resolutions reveals a sharp and sudden turn in their opinion. In their view, Wilson was a petulant and sick man and now the principal obstacle to ratification. These leaders of opinion were in utter despair and confusion. Most of them simply gave up the fight. The effect would be devastating for Democratic fortunes during the presidential campaign.

However, Wilson continued to hope that he would lead the Democrats to victory as their presidential candidate. He made plans to have his name put in nomination at the Democratic national convention and to have himself nominated by acclamation. A group of his closest friends had to tell him that it was impossible.

Meanwhile, the parliamentary phase of the struggle moved to its inexorable conclusion when the Senate took its second and final vote on the Treaty on March 19, 1920. The only hope for approval lay in the chance that enough Democrats would defy Wilson, as many friends of the League were urging them to do, to obtain a two-thirds majority for the Lodge reservations. Twenty-one Democrats did follow their consciences rather than the command from the White House, but not enough of them defected to put the Treaty across. The Treaty with the Lodge reservations failed by seven votes.

In this, the last and greatest effort of his life, did Wilson spurn the role of statesman for that of prophet? It is easy enough from our vantage point to say that, in rejecting ratification on the only possible terms and in throwing the issue into the party arena, he did not act as a statesman. It is also clear that his illness gravely impaired his perceptions of political reality and was probably the principal cause of his strategic errors.

However, when we view the situation through Wilson's eyes, his behavior seems neither irrational nor quixotic. As has been said many times, he believed that he had the overwhelming support of the people. He had gone to them many times before, and, except in 1918, with resounding success. He was confident that he, or another pro-League Democrat, could do so again in 1920.

His friends feared that he would be devastated by Harding's victory. On the contrary, he was serene and confident on the morning after the election. He told his private secretary, "The Republicans have committed suicide." To the end of his life he was confident of the ultimate outcome and of the rectitude of his own position. As he put it: "I would rather fail in a cause that will ultimately triumph than triumph in a cause that will ultimately fail."

Wilson was fundamentally right in the one great principle at stake in the Treaty fight. The most immoral thing that a nation (or individual) can do is to refuse to exercise power responsibly when it possesses it. The United States exercised the greatest economic and potentially the greatest military power in the world in 1920. At least for a time it spurned the responsibility that accompanied its power.

Moreover, Wilson was fundamentally right in the long run. As he put it in a speech on Armistice Day in 1923: "We shall inevitably be forced by the moral obligations of freedom and honor to retrieve that fatal error and assume once more the role of courage, self-respect, and helpfulness which every true American must wish to regard as our natural part in the affairs of the world."

127

The postwar version of collective security failed in the crucial tests of the 1930s, not because the Treaty of Versailles was responsible or the peacekeeping machinery of the League of Nations was defective, but because the people of Great Britain, France, and the United States were unwilling to confront aggressors with the threat of war. Consequently, a second and more terrible world conflict came in 1939, as Wilson had prophesied it would.

The American people, and other peoples, learned the lesson that Wilson taught in 1919 and 1920, but at a fearful cost. And it is Wilson the prophet and pivot of the twentieth century who survives in history, in the hopes and aspirations of mankind for a peaceful world, and in whatever ideals of international service that the American people still cherish. One thing is certain, now that nations have the power to sear virtually the entire face of the earth: The prophet of 1919–1920 was right in his vision; the challenge that he raised then is today no less real and no less urgent than it was in his own time.

Bibliographical Essay

This book is based upon the author's work over the past thirty years in private manuscript collections, governmental archives in the United States, Great Britain, France, and Germany, and other sources like newspapers. It is based also upon the monographs, biographies, and articles of a large group of colleagues who have written on Wilson and American diplomatic history and international relations in the twentieth century. Since these are all listed in William M. Leary, Jr., and Arthur S. Link's Goldentree Bibliography, *The Progressive Era and the Great War, 1896–1920* (AHM Publishing Corp., 1978), there is no need to repeat that list here. This essay is designed as a guide to readers who want to explore the best and most significant sources and literature on Wilson and his foreign policies, such as would normally be available in any good library.

The basic source is Arthur S. Link *et al.* (eds.), *The Papers of Woodrow Wilson* (Princeton, N.J., 1966–   ), thirty volumes to the spring of 1979. Volume 27 begins the presidential series. Herein are printed and annotated all important materials (gathered from personal manuscript collections and governmental archives around the world) relating to Wilson the diplomatist and his diplomatic policies.

There is not a good major one-volume biography of Wilson. The authorized biographies, Ray Stannard Baker, *Woodrow Wilson: Life and Letters,* 8 vols. (Garden City, N.Y., 1927–1939) and *Woodrow Wilson and World Settlement,* 3 vols. (Garden City, N.Y., 1923), are still useful, particularly the latter, since it was written with Wilson's collaboration.

For Wilson's foreign policies from 1913 to the outbreak of the war, the most comprehensive coverage is to be found in Arthur S. Link, *Wilson: The New Freedom* (Princeton, N.J., 1956).

The literature on Wilson and the problems of neutrality is very rich: Edward H. Buehrig, *Woodrow Wilson and the Balance of Power* (Bloomington, Ind., 1955); Patrick Devlin, *Too Proud to Fight: Woodrow Wilson's Neutrality* (New York, 1974); Arthur S. Link, *Wilson: The Struggle for Neutrality, 1914–1915* (Princeton, N.J., 1960), *Wilson: Confusions and Crises, 1915–1916* (Princeton, N.J., 1964), and *Wilson: Campaigns for Progressivism and Peace* (Princeton, N.J., 1965); and Ernest R. May, *The World War and American Isolation, 1914–1917* (Cambridge, Mass., 1959). John Milton Cooper, Jr., *The Vanity of Power: American Isolationism and World War I, 1914–1917* (Westport, Conn., 1969), is excellent for the general historical context.

The reader might be interested to compare these works, now regarded as the standard literature on the subject, with the two most prominent products of the so-called revisionist school of the 1930s: Charles C. Tansill, *America Goes to War* (Boston, 1942), and Walter Millis, *Road to War: America, 1914–1917,* (Boston and New York, 1935).

The literature on Wilson's wartime diplomacy is still somewhat sparse, but the following are essential: W. B. Fowler, *British-American Relations, 1917–1918* (Princeton, N.J., 1969); Lawrence E. Gelfand, *The Inquiry: American Preparations for Peace, 1917–1919* (Princeton, N.J., 1957); and Arno J. Mayer, *Political Origins of the New Diplomacy, 1917–1918* (New Haven, 1959).

Books on Wilson and the Paris Peace Conference are so numerous that it would be easy to overlook some important works. *Woodrow Wilson and World Settlement,* cited earlier, presents the story through Wilson's eyes. Arno J. Mayer, *The Politics of Peacemaking* (New York, 1967), discusses the European scene in panoramic fashion. N. Gordon Levin, Jr., *Woodrow Wilson and World Politics* (New York, 1968), presents an interesting thesis that becomes procrustean in its constraints. Inga Floto, *Colonel House in Paris* (Princeton, N.J., 1979), has replaced Paul Birdsall, *Versailles Twenty Years After* (New York, 1941), as the best single-volume history of the peace conference. Valuable specialized works are George W. Egerton, *Great Britain and the Creation of the League of Nations* (Chapel Hill, N.C., 1978), in which Wilson plays a large role; Herbert Hoover, *The Ordeal of*

Woodrow Wilson (New York, 1958); Carl P. Parrini, *Heir to Empire: United States Economic Diplomacy, 1916–1923* (Pittsburgh, Pa., 1969); and Seth P. Tillman, *Anglo-American Relations at the Paris Peace Conference* (Princeton, N.J., 1961).

The literature on Wilson and the Russian Revolution is very uneven. The best book is Betty Miller Unterberger's, *America's Siberian Intervention, 1918–1920* (Durham, N.C., 1956). George F. Kennan, *Russia and the West under Lenin and Stalin* (Boston, 1960), reveals keen understanding of Wilson's thinking about the Russian Revolution. The standard general work is John M. Thompson, *Russia, Bolshevism, and the Versailles Peace* (Princeton, N.J., 1966).

There is no single good book on Wilson and the Treaty fight. Denna F. Fleming, *The United States and the League of Nations, 1918–1920* (New York, 1932), is still a useful survey, but it is strongly pro-Wilson and very hard on Lodge. John A. Garraty, *Henry Cabot Lodge* (New York, 1953), also is much more balanced. One obtains a clear and dispassionate view of Republican strategy in Richard W. Leopold, *Elihu Root and the Conservative Tradition* (Boston, 1954). William Widenor, *Henry Cabot Lodge and the Search for an "American" Foreign Policy* (Berkeley, Cal., and Los Angeles, 1979), sees the treaty fight through Lodge's eyes. The best work on Wilson and the treaty fight has been done by Kurt Wimer in the following articles: "Woodrow Wilson Tries Conciliation: An Effort that Failed," *The Historian,* XXV (1963), 419–38; "Woodrow Wilson's Plan for a Vote of Confidence: An Effort that Failed," *Pennsylvania History,* XXVIII (1961), 2–16; "Woodrow Wilson's Plans to Enter the League of Nations Through an Executive Agreement," *Western Political Quarterly,* XI (1958), 800–812; and two unpublished articles. Herbert F. Margulies, *Senator Lenroot of Wisconsin* (Columbia, Mo., 1977), has established the important point that the so-called mild reservationists were really the authors of the Lodge reservations.

Edwin A. Weinstein, "Woodrow Wilson's Neurological Illness," *Journal of American History,* LV2I (1970) 324–51, is essential to an understanding of Wilson's behavior during the treaty fight, as will be his forthcoming medical biography of Wilson.

Index